A part of the

Incorporating Without a Lawyer Series

Chicago Public Library

REFERENCE

W. DEAN BROWN

ORIOLE PARK BRANCH
7454 W. BALMORAL AVE.
CHICAGO, IL. 60656

DISCARD

Copyright © 1995 - 1996
By Consumer Corporation / Consumer Publishing Corp.
All rights reserved.

R01096 10536

ORIOLE PARK BRANCH
7454 W. BALMORAL AVE.
CHICAGO, IL. 60656

DISCARD

This publication is intended to provide accurate information with regard to the subject ~~mat~~tioned that this book is sold with the understanding that the Publisher is not engaged in re~~...~~ professional service. Since everyone's situation is different, readers are urged to consult ~~...~~ advice regarding their particular needs.

Since we live in a lawsuit prone society, we feel the following disclaimer is necessary. Although we make every attempt to insure that the information contained in this book is accurate and up-to-date, we make no warranty, either expressed or implied, as to the accuracy of the information contained in this book. Neither do we make any warranty as to this book's fitness for a particular purpose or its merchantability. Consumer Corporation nor the author shall be liable for incidental or consequential damages resulting from the use of this book or the information contained herein.

Distributed in the U.S. and Canada by
Independent Publishers Group
814 North Franklin Street
Chicago, IL 60610
Bookstores and Wholesalers please call 1-800-888-4741

Published by
Consumer Publishing, Inc.
Consumer Corporation
11409 Municipal Center Drive
P.O. Box 23830
Concord, TN 37933-1830
Questions please call (615) 539-2462
Orders please call 1-800-677-2462

Consumer Corporation and Consumer Publishing, Inc.
are trademarks of Consumer Corporation.

Designed and written by Dean Brown.
Manufactured in the United States of America.

Copyright ©1994 by Consumer Corporation—All rights reserved.

THE INCORPORATING WITHOUT A LAWYER SERIES

	ISBN
Incorporating In Alabama Without A Lawyer	1-879760-05-3
Incorporating In Arkansas Without A Lawyer	1-879760-07-X
Incorporating In Arizona Without A Lawyer	1-879760-19-3
Incorporating In California Without A Lawyer	1-879760-25-8
Incorporating In Colorado Without A Lawyer	1-879760-29-0
Incorporating In Connecticut Without A Lawyer	1-879760-21-5
Incorporating In Florida Without A Lawyer	1-879760-26-6
Incorporating In Georgia Without A Lawyer	1-879760-01-0
Incorporating In Illinois Without A Lawyer	1-879760-10-X
Incorporating In Indiana Without A Lawyer	1-879760-12-6
Incorporating In Kansas Without A Lawyer	1-879760-30-4
Incorporating In Kentucky Without A Lawyer	1-879760-04-5
Incorporating In Massachusetts Without A Lawyer	1-879760-22-3
Incorporating In Maryland Without A Lawyer	1-879760-16-9
Incorporating In Michigan Without A Lawyer	1-879760-09-6
Incorporating In Minnesota Without A Lawyer	1-879760-14-2
Incorporating In Missouri Without A Lawyer	1-879760-08-8
Incorporating In Mississippi Without A Lawyer	1-879760-06-1
Incorporating In N. Carolina Without A Lawyer	1-879760-02-9
Incorporating In New Jersey Without A Lawyer	1-879760-17-7
Incorporating In New York Without A Lawyer	1-879760-28-2
Incorporating In Nevada Without A Lawyer	1-879760-23-1
Incorporating In Ohio Without A Lawyer	1-879760-11-8
Incorporating In Oklahoma Without A Lawyer	1-879760-31-2
Incorporating In Oregon Without A Lawyer	1-879760-20-7
Incorporating In Pennsylvania Without A Lawyer	1-879760-15-0
Incorporating In Tennessee Without A Lawyer	1-879760-00-2
Incorporating In Texas Without A Lawyer	1-879760-27-4
Incorporating In Utah Without A Lawyer	1-879760-18-5
Incorporating In Virginia Without A Lawyer	1-879760-03-7
Incorporating In Washington Without A Lawyer	1-879760-24-X
Incorporating In Washington D.C. Without A Lawyer	1-879760-33-9
Incorporating In Wisconsin Without A Lawyer	1-879760-13-4

CONTENTS

PART ONE:
BEFORE YOU INCORPORATE

CHAPTER 1
—*The background of corporations*
—*How a lawyer incorporates a business*

CHAPTER 2
—*Definition*
—*Officers, directors, shareholders, and their roles*
—*How a corporation works*

CHAPTER 3
—*The difference between a business with one owner, a partnership, and a corporation*
—*Liability*
—*Tax advantages*
—*Corporate pension plans*
—*Medical insurance*
—*Medical reimbursement plans*
—*Life insurance*

CHAPTER 4
—*Cash*
—*Accounts receivable*
—*Notes receivable*
—*Miscellaneous assets*
—*Assets with titles or deeds*
—*Liabilities*
—*Other contracts*
—*Partnership agreements*

CHAPTER 5
—*Answers to the most common incorporating questions*

PART TWO:
AFTER YOU INCORPORATE

PART THREE:
HOW TO INCORPORATE

This edition is dedicated

to the thousands of wonderful readers who have called

or written just to say thanks.

ABOUT THE AUTHOR

Dean Brown graduated with honors from the University of Tennessee in 1985, with a Bachelor of Science Degree in Accounting. After graduation, he worked for the small business services division of Price Waterhouse, one of the largest public accounting firms in the world. Here, the author worked to help small business owners find better ways to operate their business. Working with these small business organizations made him aware that small businesses operate on small budgets.

Unfortunately, no matter how great the benefits of incorporating are, most small business people can't afford to pay a professional to incorporate their business, and most don't know how to do it themselves. To fill this need, a series of how-to-incorporate books was started. Brown has since written over thirty books on the subject.

He makes his home in Knoxville, Tennessee where he writes, operates Consumer Publishing, and occasionally lecturers at the University of Tennessee School of Business. He loves spending time in the nearby Great Smoky Mountains with his wife Cherie, and his two daughters, Mallory and Amber.

My story

I'd like to take a minute to tell you a story, the story of this book. I find the more I know about a book or a book's author, the more enjoyable it is for me. By reading this short story, I hope you will better appreciate why this book is here.

I've never been satisfied with the status quo. I believe that no matter how things are being done today, there is probably a better way. Things that don't work properly frustrate me, and when something frustrates me, I do something about it. My frustration with the legal system started in 1988 when I hired my first lawyer. A local company reneged on a contract, and decided to keep the $12,000 they owed me. At the time, I didn't know my way around the courthouse, much less how to sue someone. So, I felt that hiring an attorney was my only alternative. Like you, I'm the kind of person who likes to do things for myself. It irritated me that I was cheated by this big corporation, and the only thing I could do was hire a stranger to fight my battle for me. To make a long story short, two years later I got my money. Well, about half of it anyway. My lawyer got the rest.

Oddly enough, the same year my lawsuit was settled I found myself working for a law firm. Since the managing partner was also a CPA, the firm specialized in business law and accounting. My education is in accounting, with a concentration in business law, so I managed the accounting work for the firm. Since incorporating offers tremendous tax breaks to a business, incorporating was a common, even routine procedure for the firm. The paperwork was usually handled by the accounting department.

Knowing how easy it is to incorporate a business, and remembering my own experience with lawyers, it often upset me to see clients being charged hundreds of dollars to have their name and address put on a form. I knew that these people could do it themselves if they only knew how. "Someone needs to write a book", I often thought. Then one day it hit me. Lawyers don't charge for what they do. They charge for what they know! They are simply selling us information. They go to law school, study our laws, then charge hundreds of dollars to tell us how they work!

That day, I decided to write my first book, a thin 50 page volume called *Incorporating In Tennessee Without A Lawyer*. It took three months of hard work to complete, and was published by Consumer Publishing, my own company. Since then, I've written over thirty manuals for various states and helped thousands of people save money by incorporating their own business. This book is in your hands today because I decided to right a wrong. I decided to do something to help the little guy. In a country where government is by the people, for the people, and of the people, I can't believe that we have to pay someone up to $500 per hour to have our own laws explained to us.

Starting a business of your own is not an easy thing to do. But as they say, nothing worth having is easy to get. I hope that through this book I can make the experience a little easier for you.

Thank you for giving me the chance to help.

INTRODUCTION - PLEASE READ

I would like to thank the many people at the State Capitol, the IRS, and the Small Business Administration for providing the information needed to make this book possible.

Everything possible to insure the accuracy of this material has been done, but please understand that laws and procedures are constantly changing, and are subject to different interpretations. Since we live in such a litigious society, Consumer Publishing, Inc., the author, nor anyone associated with this book makes any guarantee or warranty about the information it contains, or information obtained through the telephone help line. Furthermore, the state after which this book is entitled is not responsible for its contents. The responsibility of starting and running a corporation rests with you. Use of this book and related information constitutes your agreement with this disclaimer.

If you experience any difficulty, or encounter any changes, please let us know so that we may assist you and keep our books updated. This book is not designed to give legal or tax advice, and the material contained herein should not be viewed as such. If you feel you need the services of a professional, you should seek them.

Forms

This book was constructed so the pages could be removed easily, similar to a "scratch pad". The forms are as easily removed from this book as a sheet is torn from a scratch pad. All you need to do is open the book to the page you wish to remove. Then, while holding that page, open the book as far as possible until the front and back covers are touching each other, and gently pull your form out. If you have difficulty removing any pages, or damage any while removing them, please call us and replacements will be sent immediately.

Before you attempt to complete any forms, you may want to make a couple of copies of the form first. This way, you'll have extras if you make a mistake. You will definitely need to make copies of the forms in chapter eight, because you will use these pages in keeping records for the corporation and will need extras as time goes by.

Copyright

This entire work is protected by copyright. Most of the forms, and all of the systems used in this book are unique and were developed by the author to help you incorporate your own business. Copyright infringements will be enjoined and reparations will be sought from infringers. Only the purchaser of this book may make copies of its pages, and such copies may only be for corporations in which the purchaser will be an officer, director, or shareholder. Since all papers filed with the state are open for public review, our copyrights are easily enforced.

Libraries

If you are borrowing this book from your local library, *please do not copy any of the forms or use the stock certificates.* You can purchase a copy at your local bookstore or from us at 1-800-677-2462. Please understand that sales of this book make it possible for people to provide for their families, much the same as you are trying to do with your business. Book sales also make it possible for us to continue publishing these manuals. Sure you'll spend $24.95, but that's a small price to pay compared to paying a lawyer several hundred dollars. Thank you for understanding.

Professionals

If you are a lawyer, or other professional, please understand that this book was written to help small business people. It was not written to teach you how to incorporate their businesses for a fee. Please refer your clients to your bookstore.

Many professionals, especially CPA's and independent paralegals, help small business people by telling their clients about the book, or actually selling a copy to them. Professionals that sell our books to their clients buy several copies at a time at a discounted price. By doing this, they act much like a bookstore with one important difference. They can be there to help their client through the process. Also, by selling the book to their clients, they greatly reduce the chance of being prosecuted for "practicing law without a license". If you are interested in offering these books to your clients, please contact the Special Sales Division of our distributor, Independent Publishers Group. Their office is in Chicago and their telephone number is (312) 337-0747, or toll free 1-800-888-4741.

Drop me a line!

I wrote this book to help small business people save money and get off to a successful start. Since then, thousands of people have saved millions of dollars in legal fees by using my books. If you feel this book has helped you, please drop me a note or a post card of your hometown to let me know? Please send them to:

Dean Brown
Consumer Publishing Inc.
P.O. Box 23830
Concord, TN 37933-1830   *Thank you for buying this book.*

1

INCORPORATING WITH A LAWYER

Most people think incorporating a business is a difficult and complex thing to do. Actually, incorporating a business is very simple. The incorporating process basically consists of two parts. The first part is deciding whether or not to incorporate, and the second part is completing the paperwork. It's that simple.

Until the early 1900's, incorporating wasn't so easy. When the first corporations were formed, a business owner had to petition the state legislature to pass a special law allowing the business to operate as a corporation. Needless to say, incorporating was a business option available only to the rich and powerful, those with enough money and influence to have such a preferential law passed. Of course, having your own special law passed was a complicated process, a process that required someone familiar with laws—a lawyer. This is how lawyers became involved with business corporations.

As the popularity of incorporating grew, state legislatures found that they spent more and more of their time incorporating businesses, and less time governing the state. To remedy this problem, states passed blanket incorporating laws under which anyone could incorporate their business by simply filing a document with the state. Making it easier to incorporate a business gave the legislatures more time for important matters, and the various taxes and incorporating fees produced generous revenues. Most states had passed these special incorporating laws by the turn of the century.

Delaware was the leader in this movement, even allowing a corporation to be formed with a single shareholder. Despite its small size, Delaware has chartered hundreds of thousands of corporations. In the 60's and 70's, other states followed Delaware's lead, reducing the incorporating process to the filing of a simple, one page form. It's unfortunate, but this chain of events is probably news to most people, even though it happened decades ago. Most people are unaware that incorporating a business is this easy. Getting a driver's license is probably as difficult, but teenagers do it everyday. You know that getting a drivers license is an easy thing to do. The problem is, no one told you that incorporating was easy until I did. I've found that you get what you expect in life. If you expect incorporating to be difficult, you can easily find someone to tell you that it is. Just ask any lawyer. On the other hand, if you believe me when I tell you that incorporating is easy, read this book, and I'll prove it to you.

Incorporating with a lawyer is an unusual chapter title for this book. In the next few paragraphs, I'll describe the process of having a lawyer incorporate your business. I'm doing this because I want to give you an overview of the process, and show you what goes on inside a lawyer's office. Also, I want to show you that you're not missing anything. You'll soon see that this book can do everything a lawyer can do, except type the forms for you.

Corporate Lawyers Only Please

If you want a lawyer to incorporate your business, the first thing you'll need to do is find a lawyer. Finding a lawyer to sue your employer for injuries sustained while on the job is an easy thing to do. All you have to do is watch television. Lawyers are on every channel promising that "someone will pay for your pain and suffering". Finding a good corporate lawyer is slightly more difficult, because they only advertise in the yellow pages, the best place to look. This brings up an important distinction. Not every lawyer knows how to incorporate a business. There are so many different facets to our law, that no lawyer is proficient in all of them. Some specialized areas of "practice" are tax law, criminal law, patent law, divorce or "family" law, Social Security Law, real estate law, personal injury law, immigration law, bankruptcy law, contract law and of course—corporate law.

At this point you're probably, saying, "Don't all lawyers learn how to incorporate a business in law school?" Well, no. There are so many different areas of law, that a law school can't cover every subject in sufficient detail. Upon graduation, law students choose the area or areas of law in which they will specialize. At this point, a new "corporate" lawyer will study the process of incorporating.

By the way, lawyers learn how to incorporate a business the same way you do, by reading books, and asking the state a few questions. Lawyers have special books for this. They're called "practice forms books". These special books are written by lawyers for lawyers, and are available only to lawyers. Practice forms books lead a new corporate lawyer step-by-step through the incorporating process in his state. What a concept! They explain in minute detail how to interview the client, what to discuss, and how to complete the necessary forms. They even devote an entire section on how to properly bill the client—complete with a sample bill. Everyone learns about the incorporating process the same way, from books.

The First Meeting

After you've found a lawyer specializing in corporate law, you'll set up an initial appointment with him, and go to his office. In your first meeting, the lawyer should spend some time explaining what a corporation is; the pros and cons of incorporating; what incorporating will do for you; whether to be an "S" or a "C" corporation; and answer your questions about incorporating. If you are incorporating an existing corporation, the lawyer should spend some time discussing the special considerations of incorporating an existing business. If you look at the table of contents, you'll see this book covers these topics in part one.

After this discussion, the lawyer will gather the information needed to prepare the paperwork. This information will include the names of the directors, shareholders, officers, the name of the corporation, and how the stock will be distributed. At this point, your first meeting should end. That's right, your first meeting. After your first meeting, the paperwork will be "prepared", and filed with the state. When the paperwork has returned from the state, you will meet with the lawyer a second time to hold an organizational meeting and issue the stock of the corporation. This second meeting will be discussed later.

After your first meeting, the lawyer will check to see if the name you like is being used by another corporation. If it is not already being used, the paperwork can be prepared. The lawyer has two options for preparing paperwork. He can either prepare the paperwork using the examples in his practice forms book, or order a "corporate kit" from a legal supply company. A corporate kit is an impressive corporate records book that includes pre-prepared corporate forms for your state, stock certificates imprinted with the corporate name, and a corporate seal. These books cost about $60, and are very nice. Most lawyers use corporate kits. The lawyer will sign the required paperwork for you and forward it to the state, where it is filed. This process is covered in part three.

At this point, I want to make a note about what goes on between your meetings with the lawyer. The name check, the preparation of the paperwork, etc. is usually done by the lawyer's secretary or assistant. The legal forms books used by most lawyers encourage them to delegate these "routine" duties to their assistant, thereby allowing the lawyer to make better use of his time. *Webster's Legal Secretary's Handbook*, published by the *Webster's Dictionary* people, devotes an entire section to "the steps that a legal secretary can take in creating a corporation". Webster knows who does the incorporating paperwork!

The Second Meeting

After your paperwork has returned from the state, you will meet with your lawyer for a second time. At this time you will review the paperwork, hold an organizational meeting, and issue the stock of the corporation. An organizational meeting is held to formally organize the corporation. At this meeting, the corporation's charter, and bylaws will be formally adopted, and the directors and officers of the corporation will be officially appointed. Stock of the corporation will be issued at this time, and you will be presented with a stock certificate. If the meeting is done "correctly", there will be motions made, motions seconded, motions voted on, and resolutions passed. This meeting, or any corporate meeting for that matter, are what I call "rain dances". They're often over formalized for effect. It's a fascinating show, but what good does it do? Holding an organizational meeting is covered in chapter ten.

During this second meeting, the matter of "S" corporation status should also be discussed. Since this subject is actually a tax matter and not part of the state's incorporating requirements, it may not be covered at all. In any case, the lawyer should outline the benefits of "S" corporation status, and if he is proficient in tax law, help decide what's best for you. However, unless your lawyer is a CPA, you should discuss the matter with your CPA or tax advisor.

After all the formalities are out of the way, the lawyer should spend some time discussing a few things you'll need to know in order to operate your corporation. This will include things like record keeping, how to hold a directors meeting, and what to do if someone wants to buy more stock.

Lawyers I know prefer that clients know nothing about the formalities of operating a corporation. This way, the client will need to seek the lawyer's advice on all corporate matters. This provides an annuity for the lawyer. Every time the owner needs a little help, the help comes with a bill. I know of corporations that even hold director and shareholder meetings at the lawyer's office. The lawyer makes sure they do everything "right", and charges them $100 an hour.

At this point, your meetings are over and you're finished incorporating. The forms are filed and hopefully, you know a little more about corporations than you did before. There's only one problem, the bill. Everyday, I talk to people across the country, and they tell me how much lawyers in their area charge to incorporate a business. It astounds me that some lawyers charge up to $2000. I have found that lawyers familiar with the incorporating process charge less, usually around $500.

I used to work with a lawyer who joked that he "charged by the pound". The heavier the pile of paperwork, the more he could charge. You see, aside from the "rain dances" the paperwork is the only evidence that any work was actually done. The more paperwork, the easier it is to justify a high fee. After you see what little "paperwork" is actually involved, you'll wonder how a $500 fee could be justified.

Well, so much for incorporating with a lawyer. Now, let's learn how to incorporate your business without one. The rest of this book is organized to follow the process outlined in this chapter. In part one, you'll learn some background information about corporations and how they work. In part two, you'll learn what you need to know after you've incorporated, things like IRS forms and record keeping. Part three will lead you step-by-step through the paperwork.

2

WHAT IS A CORPORATION?

Basically, a corporation is an artificial person created and "brought to life" by filing a form known as the articles of incorporation with the state of your choice. Its a person like you and me—but only on paper. This newly created "person" is a separate and distinct entity from the people who own and control it—its shareholders. A corporation enjoys many of the rights and privileges that people do. Among other things, a corporation can own and operate businesses, make contracts, own property, sue, and be sued.

Since it's a person in all legal respects, a corporation has the ability to act for, or on the behalf of its owners. The nature of the corporation allows a group of business owners act as one, much the way a partnership does, with one important advantage. Since the corporation is a separate legal entity capable of being sued, it can protect its owners by taking the heat if something goes wrong.

Directors

Although it is a legal "person" with rights of its own, a corporation can't walk, talk, think, or act for itself. It can't hold a pen to sign contracts. It can't go to the bank to make a deposit. It can't market its products or perform any of the physical tasks required to operate a business. Since it has no mental or physical capabilities, the business affairs of the corporation are managed and "directed" by directors. The body of directors that oversee a corporation's activities are know as "the board of directors". Directors are like the guardians of an incompetent adult who has rights, but can't think or act for himself. Directors meet from time to time to plan and approve actions the corporation will take to conduct its business.

Following correct procedure, directors are like trustees, charged by law to oversee the business affairs of the corporation. More like special consultants who come in periodically to plan and approve corporate actions, directors are usually not employees of the corporation. In return for their efforts, directors usually receive a token compensation, and other perks.

Deviating from the procedure envisioned by state law, the directors of large corporations don't actually oversee the business affairs of the corporation. In these corporations, directors are usually well known business people, celebrities, or former politicians who lend credibility to the corporation. In this case, being a director is more a position of status and the "directors" merely meet from time to time to "rubber stamp" what the officers they appointed have decided is best for the corporation. This rubber stamp approval of corporate action is not the correct procedure, but is reality in many cases.

Officers

Although directors are responsible for managing and directing the business affairs of the corporation, they mostly oversee the "big picture". To manage the day to day activities of the corporation, the directors appoint and hire officers. Officers handle all of the daily decisions required to run a business, and the scope of their duties usually depends on the size of the corporation.

That is, the president of a corporation like Sears probably delegates the important duty of selecting new store sites to a subordinate, merely checking in periodically to make sure things are running smoothly. In contrast, the presidential duties of a small business corporation would probably include everything from selecting the store location, to selling the merchandise. A corporation usually has the following officers:

A President—who carries out the most important functions.

A Vice-President—who can act for the President when needed.

A Secretary—who is responsible for corporate records and meetings.

A Treasurer—who manages the financial affairs of the corporation.

When managing the daily activities of the corporation, the president is generally responsible for the more important or glamorous responsibilities like signing contracts or developing strategies for the corporation. The vice-president fills in for the president when necessary, or assists the president. The secretary maintains corporate records and correlates the organizational affairs of the corporation. The treasurer is responsible for the financial welfare of the corporation, from obtaining loans, to overseeing the accounting department. Although large corporations can delegate duties the way state laws intended, the officer positions of a small corporation are usually filled by a single person who will carry out most, or all of these responsibilities.

Many times, in a small corporation, the directors and the officers are actually the same people who simply "wear different hats". That is, when you're carrying out director responsibilities, you're a director, and when taking care of officer duties, you're an officer. Officers are most always employees of the corporation. Being an employee of your own corporation is important because it makes you eligible for lucrative employee benefits, like retirement plans and hospitalization insurance. These benefits are of course paid for by the corporation.

Shareholders

Now you know what roles the directors and officers play, but the most important players in the average corporation aren't the directors or the officers. The most important people are those for whom the corporation was formed - the stockholders. The stockholders are the people who started, and own the corporation for their mutual benefit. The stockholders invest money, property, or something else of value into the corporation. In return, the stockholders will own a part of the corporation relative to the amount they invested. These people provide the means by which the corporation is able to begin operating.

To provide evidence of their ownership and investment, the corporation will issue these individuals a stock certificate. That's why these people are called "stockholders". These stocks represent ownership in a particular corporation, and are similar to those bought and sold on the stock exchanges in New York. In fact, stocks of small corporations sometimes trade just as fervently as those on Wall Street. Of course, only the stocks of larger corporations are traded on an exchange.

Since we couldn't have a corporation without them, the stockholders are at the top of the power structure. They control the corporation for their common good by appointing the directors who will oversee the activities of the corporation. Ideally, in large corporations where shareholders are spread over a large geographic area, the directors are like independent observers appointed by the shareholders to help insure their interests are protected.

Of course, what's been described here is the textbook example of how a large corporation works, and is very different from how a small one works. However, all of this needed to be explained so that you might gain a fuller understanding of all the participants in the corporate world. You may understand the process better by reviewing the diagram on the next page. Your corporation will look and function exactly like this diagram. Shareholders will start the corporation by giving money or property in exchange for its stock. The shareholders will then appoint directors to monitor their investment. Finally, since being a director isn't a full time calling, the directors appoint and hire officers to actually run the corporation on a daily basis.

Your corporation, however, will have one very important difference. Most or all of these positions will be held by only one or two people.

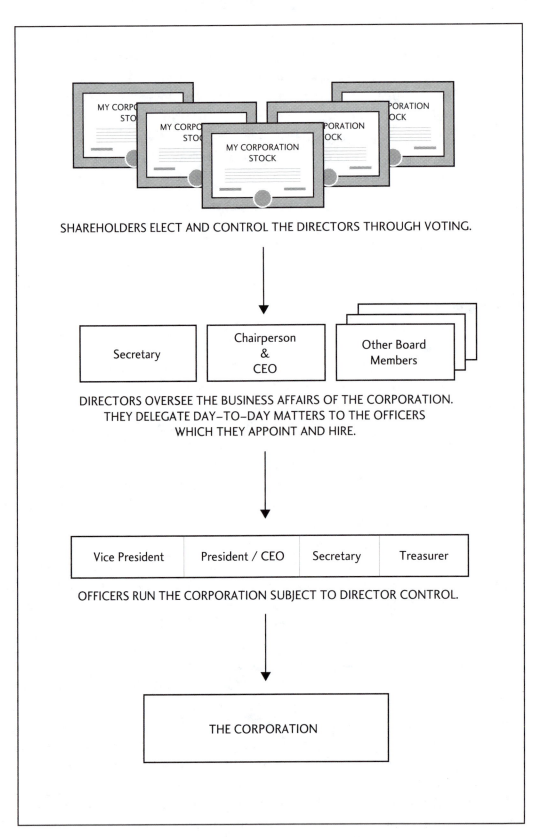

3

WHAT WILL INCORPORATING DO FOR ME?

For the answer to this question to have meaning, one must understand a few basic principles about how businesses are structured. The most common small business structures are the "sole proprietorship" and the "partnership". Other than some bookkeeping differences, these two forms of organizing a business are basically the same, with the exception of the number of people involved. The sole proprietorship is, as the name suggests, one person. The partnership is comprised of two or more people.

The sole proprietorship and the partnership differ from the corporation because the sole proprietorship and the partnership are inseparable from the owner of the business. They are one in the same. In the previous discussion, we learned that the corporation is an entity separate and distinct from its owners created to "take the heat" for them. However, in the case of the sole proprietorship and the partnership, the owner *is* the business, and business *is* the owner.

For example, if William Brown owns an unincorporated business called Brown Advertising, the legal name of the business is actually "William Brown, doing business as (dba) Brown Advertising". The name "Brown Advertising" is only an alias for William Brown himself, an alter ego if you will. If something happens to William, this Brown Advertising would actually cease to exist.

However, if William leaves the business assets to his daughters Mallory and Amber, Brown Advertising could be reborn as a new company operated by them. This time, the company could be known as Mallory Brown and Amber Brown, dba Brown Advertising. This would technically and legally be a new company. The new owners will have to open a new bank account and obtain a new tax identification number from the Internal Revenue Service for the "new" business.

I've found that it's easier to understand something when it's presented visually. So, here's another diagram, this one to show how the sole proprietorship and the partnership function. As you can see, both of these forms of business ownership function more like an extension of the owner or owners.

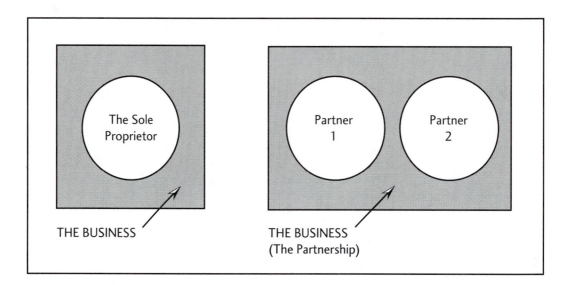

As you can see, the business and the person(s) owning the business are the same, the business being sort of a shell around the owner. In contrast, as you'll recall, the corporation is separate entity, distinct from all those who own and control it. As we'll soon see, this separation of the owners from the business is very advantageous.

When a business is not incorporated, the inseparability of the business from the owner is the cause of two major problems:

1. Since you are the business, whoever sues the business, sues you.

2. Since you are the business, you are the employer. Since the IRS only allows employees to participate in employee benefit plans, you lose some very lucrative benefits.

Incorporating basically solves both of these problems. Separating the owner (the shareholder) from the business protects him. Since the corporation has the right to sue and be sued, the person bringing a lawsuit will typically sue the corporation. In such a case, the stockholder is not sued. The corporation is sued. This is usually the case even when the owner is the only shareholder, the only director, and an officer. For example, if someone sues Ford Motor Company, the person bringing the suit will simply sue the corporation, and Mr. Ford should hardly be involved at all.

As far as employee benefits are concerned, incorporating allows you to participate as an employee and let the corporation "pick up the tab" for your benefits. You see, when your business is incorporated, the corporation (a separate entity) is the employer—not you. You just happen to be the owner of the corporation that you work for. Obviously, this is an advantageous position to be in.

How do you become an employee of your corporation? Most people simply hire themselves as officers of the corporation. Officers are usually employees of the corporation. As an employee, you can participate in employee benefit programs. The forms accompanying this book were designed to make the officers of the corporation its first employees, making them eligible for employee benefits. This strategy works for all other family members as well.

As discussed above, operating your business as a corporation offers you many advantages. Among these advantages, the personal tax breaks you'll enjoy, and the tax dollars you'll save are the best. In this section we'll briefly discuss some of the most profitable tax saving strategies available.

TAX STRATEGIES

You will need to discuss these strategies with your tax professional. No matter what, investigate these options. If your tax planner doesn't know about them, or how they work, look until you find one who does.

While larger corporations offer these perks to attract and keep good employees, the owners of small corporations do it to obtain IRS approved tax-free benefits. The best tax saving strategies are those that allow you to personally acquire fringe benefits that your corporation pays for. Why? Because this way you gain very lucrative perks without incurring personal tax liabilities. For providing you with these perks, your corporation gets a tax deduction, lowering it's tax bill.

Entire books have been written on the subject of corporate tax breaks. Instead of duplicating the efforts of others, I'll only summarize how they work. Although there are a dozen strategies that utilize this principal, here are the four most beneficial:

- A Pension Plan

- A Medical Reimbursement Plan

- Medical Insurance

- A "Free" Life Insurance Plan

Corporate Pension Plans

Most everyone is familiar with pension plans. They are the company sponsored retirement accounts that most large companies, and increasingly more smaller companies offer to their employees. Pension plans basically come in two types, either "defined benefit" plans, or "defined contribution" plans. A defined benefit plan is one that allows you to contribute different amounts each year, but pays you a set, or "defined" amount at retirement. Just the opposite, a defined contribution plan is one that requires the same fixed contribution each year, but pay out upon retirement is based on a flexible schedule.

The best thing about a pension plan is that the contributions made to your account by your corporation are tax deductions for the corporation, but are not taxable to you until you retire. These contributions earn interest and multiply with no tax implications to you, while the corporation's tax bill is lowered by thousands of dollars per year. If you have an S corporation, making these contributions lowers your personal tax bill while putting large amounts away for your retirement. It's kind of like an IRA without the small annual limit.

If you operate as a C corporation, things can be even more lucrative. You can actually borrow money from the corporate pension plan if certain, easy to meet, requirements are satisfied. Why would you want to borrow your own money? Well, first of all, it's not actually your money - not yet. It is money held in trust by your corporation for your retirement. It's not actually yours until the company writes you a check, at which point you'll have to give the IRS about a third for income taxes. But until then, you can still use the money without paying taxes on it! That's the best thing about borrowing from your own pension fund - the ability to use the money now, without incurring a tax liability. Since this money is being loaned to you, it's not income, and not taxable.

Of course, as with any loan, you'll have to pay interest. Otherwise, the IRS will consider it income, and you'll have to pay taxes on the full amount. I know you're tempted to say, "Wait a minute! What's the use if I have to pay interest"? Consider this, interest is cheaper than income taxes, and while you'll never see the money paid for income taxes again, the money you pay as interest on a loan from your pension fund, will be see again at retirement. The interest you'll pay is paid to your pension fund, making the amount available at retirement even larger. Money paid in taxes will probably be spent for a shiny new B-2 bomber, not your retirement.

So, the bottom line is that you should borrow from your pension fund as often as possible. This way, you'll get to use cash without paying taxes on it, and the interest you'll pay only makes your pension fund larger. Unfortunately, you can't borrow from your pension fund anytime you please.

You can only borrow from your pension plan to:

1. Acquire, construct, or reconstruct your personal residence

2. Pay college tuition, or

3. To pay for medical treatment requiring "immediate, heavy financial need"

It is also important to note that loans must be made available to all participants in the pension plan. Of course, with a small business, the participants are usually family members anyway.

As with any loan, you'll have to get permission to borrow the money from the organization in charge of it, the corporation, a separate and distinct entity. However, getting the approval is an easy thing to do when you own the corporation. Formal approval can be granted by the directors of the corporation. To make it official, you'll need to hold a directors meeting and keep minutes on one of the forms in chapter eight. The minutes should be written basically as follows:

"It has been decided by the board of directors of (corporation name) to entitle employees of the corporation, specifically (your name) to borrow funds from the corporate pension plan. The proceeds of this loan will be used in accordance with Internal Revenue Code § 72. Terms and conditions for borrowing will be similar to those at local lending institutions and the interest rate may not exceed that allowed by state law. A promissory note will be executed and filed with the corporation."

All directors must sign and date this form showing their affirmative vote on the matter. Also, whoever is managing your pension fund, a stockbroker, bank trust department, etc., will need a copy of this resolution. Finally, remember to consult your CPA about this, as he will be up to date on the IRS requirements and has probably done it before.

Free Medical Insurance

One of the best things about having a corporation is letting the corporation pay the premiums for your medical, and dental insurance. Again, these benefits are generally not taxable to you, and don't come out of your paycheck. Letting the corporation pay for your medical insurance provides you with expensive benefits, while providing a tax deduction for the corporation.

Since an "S" corporation flows its deductions to the shareholder's personal tax return, only a percentage of health insurance premiums are deductible. If you want to take full advantage of having your corporation pay your health insurance premiums, it will be better to operate as a "C" corporation. Also, the corporation must deduct these payments through a medical reimbursement plan to meet IRS approval.

Medical Reimbursement Plans

A medical reimbursement plan is an employee benefit plan that allows the corporation to reimburse you for expenses incurred for insurance payments and deductibles, insurance co-payments, eyeglasses, braces, and so on. You're probably beginning to see how beneficial a plan like this could be. Each year, we spend thousands of dollars on these items that even the best insurance doesn't pay for. Fortunately, when your business is incorporated, you can let the corporation pick up the tab for these expensive items.

A medical reimbursement plan like this can save the shareholder thousands of dollars per year, and provide the corporation a tax deduction. You will need to hold a directors meeting on the matter and let the minutes show that the directors approve and adopt the medical reimbursement plan. A medical reimbursement plan is a standard fill in the blank type form that can be found in many office supply stores. A medical reimbursement plan and the forms used to adopt the plan are included in the corporate outfits show on the last two pages of the book.

Free Life Insurance

The IRS allows a corporation to pay premiums for life insurance for its employees up to $50,000 in death benefits for each employee. Since the premiums for term life insurance for a younger person are low, this may not seem like much of a benefit, but to older business people, the amount can be substantial. This insurance plan can be quite profitable. Besides, it's "free" so take advantage of it. All you'll need to do, like you'll need to do every time the corporation does something important, is to hold a meeting where the directors approve of taking the action and record the results on a MINUTES OF DIRECTORS MEETING form found in chapter eight.

4

INCORPORATING AN EXISTING BUSINESS

Since an existing business has employees, leases, existing liabilities, bank accounts and other contractual arrangements, incorporating a preexisting business is not quite as simple as incorporating a new one. It's more complicated and will take more time. It's more than simply changing stationery.

Because a corporation is a separate and distinct entity and not simply an extension of the owner, incorporating an existing business is not as simple as just changing the name and doing business as usual. After incorporating, the corporation will actually be doing business with your customers, selling your products, making your loan payments and so on.

If you wish to conduct business as a corporation, the corporation will, in effect, need to "take your place" and formally adopt all contracts you've undertaken to conduct business. In some cases, the corporation may simply ratify the contracts that you have entered. In other cases, the old contracts will need to be voided and new ones entered into. In any case, the business that you have known and operated in the past will legally cease to exist, and the corporation will take its place as a totally new entity. It's almost as if you sold your business and its assets to the corporation.

Actually, if you transfer all your company's assets to the new corporation, you have, in effect, "sold" your business and its assets to the corporation. For this, the corporation will pay you with its stock. When this happens, the corporation basically owns your business, and you own the stock of the corporation. This is how you become separated from your business, thus gaining personal liability protection, and generous tax benefits.

Now that you understand the basics of incorporating a preexisting business, we need to discuss some of the details you'll need to consider when incorporating. However, at this point a word of caution is in order. Incorporating a preexisting business is a fairly straightforward event, but if you don't have a working knowledge of contracts and business law, you may be asking for trouble by going it alone.

Before beginning this process, you may want to do some research on contract law. Many books on the subject are available at your local bookstore or library. Also, your CPA is a good source of information. CPA's have formal training in business law and contracts, and your's may be able to help. As a last resort, you may want to consider hiring an experienced lawyer.

Please understand that this book was written to help you incorporate a business without a lawyer. Since incorporating an existing business includes areas of law beyond the scope of this book, some of which could take volumes to explain, an attempt to fully cover these areas will not be made. This is merely a basic outline of things you'll need to consider when incorporating an existing business, and is in no way to be considered a complete discourse on the subject, or a how to manual. Also, please remember that transferring property to a corporation may have tax implications, and you should see your CPA before doing anything.

When incorporating an existing business, you must first formally dissolve the old business. Any property held by the existing business will again be held by you personally. After you regain title to the property, there are basically two ways of proceeding:

1. You can keep some of the property in your name personally, or

2. You can simply transfer everything to the corporation.

If you choose to keep some of the business assets in your name, you may do so for the following reasons:

1. To help maintain control when you are not the only shareholder, and

2. To receive personal income at a lower tax rate.

In a corporation where you are not the only shareholder, it is important to retain as much control over the corporation as possible. One way of exercising control is through your voting stock. Another way is to control the assets that the corporation needs to operate. Simply stated, when the equipment needed to operate is under your control, you will usually be treated more fairly by other shareholders because you have the ability to "take your equipment and go home" when things don't go your way.

Secondly, keeping property out of the corporation can be very tax advantageous, especially if your salary income is high. When you retain title to property the corporation needs to operate, you can lease the property back to the corporation, and in return, receive lease payments. You can then lower the taxable effect of these lease payments with depreciation and other expenses related to the property's operation.

Usually, when a preexisting business is incorporated, everything, or most everything, is transferred to the corporation. This might include all the company assets, liabilities, and other contracts. Assets are usually transferred by conveying your title in them to the corporation. Liabilities, and other contracts are transferred to the corporation when the corporation formally adopts them.

Basically, you will "transfer and assign all your rights" in an item to the corporation with a written agreement stating that you do so. If the item has a title or deed, new documents must be prepared to show that the corporation now legally owns it.

The corporation must then formally adopt and approve everything that is done. To do this you will need to prepare director's consents to corporate action stating that the directors "approve and adopt" everything that is done. Also, if deeds or titles are involved, the corporation president will sign the documents needed to transfer the assets to the corporation. If you "transfer" all your business assets to your corporation, you should do so in return for the stock that the corporation will issue to you. This way, you will reduce or eliminate any chance that the transfers will cause tax problems. Assets to be transferred will include things like:

- Cash in the bank

- Accounts receivable (Money your customers owe)

- Notes receivable (Other monies owed)

- Inventory

- Prepaid Expenses (Insurance)

- Deposits

- Cars and other vehicles

- Plant equipment & machinery

- Office equipment & computers

- Buildings

- Land

29

Cash

Transferring cash is an easy thing to do. It's done by opening a new bank account in the name of the corporation, and putting the cash from your old account into the corporation's. You will actually close your old account and transfer all the funds with a check made payable to the corporation. You will then be authorized by corporate resolution to write checks on this new account. You will no longer "own" this money, because the corporation will.

However, by owning the stock of the corporation, you still indirectly "own" the money. However, you will no longer be able to dip into this cash whenever you please, because it now is the property of the corporation. But don't worry, the tax advantages gained by incorporating will make it worth the inconvenience.

Accounts Receivable

Accounts receivable is a formal contractual agreement between you and your customers in which they promise to pay you for goods and services provided to them. Since your business has actually ceased to exist, you'll need to assign your "rights" to collect this money to the corporation. All monies received in the future should be deposited into the corporate account, and you should notify your customers to make their checks payable to the corporation. This is a good chance to let your customers know that you have incorporated your business.

Notes Receivable

Notes receivable are like accounts receivable, except that notes receivable usually have promissory notes to back them up. For example, if you own a car lot where you sometimes finance your customer's purchases, your customers will sign a note promising to pay a fixed amount of money at certain intervals. When these promissory notes were made, they were made on behalf of your old business, which no longer exists. Therefore, you'll need to "assign the rights to collect payments" to the corporation, and similarly, tell the borrowers to make their payments to the corporation.

Miscellaneous Assets

Miscellaneous assets like inventory, prepaid expenses, office furniture, computers, and deposits are usually transferred to the corporation when the stock is issued. Documentation will include a listing in the corporate records that the property is being transferred to the corporation in exchange for corporate stock. For things like computers, and other small, yet expensive items, you will also need to give the corporation a "Bill of Sale" so that the corporation may prove it has legal title to the property. This is necessary to enable the corporation to sell the item in the future.

Assets With Titles or Deeds

Some assets, like cars, machinery, buildings, and other larger items, have a title or a deed that shows who legally owns them. The titles and/or deeds to these items will need to be redone and re-filed in the name of the corporation. This may involve lawyers, title companies, and local governments, all of which will cost you time and money. However, for reasons listed above, these are sometimes not transferred to the corporation.

Liabilities

For a minute, lets discuss the other side of the balance sheet, the liabilities side. Before incorporating, you are personally responsible for all your business's liabilities and loans. Since you now want your corporation to make these payments, the corporation will need to formally adopt the debts as its own. To do this, you will need to meet with your banker and other creditors to arrange for the notes and other liabilities to become the corporation's.

At best, the creditors will totally release you from the debts in exchange for new promissory notes signed by the corporation. This is best for you, because you will no longer be responsible for the payments, and your personal assets will probably not be taken to collect the debts.

In reality however, the creditors will not only want you to stay on the notes, but they will also insist that the corporation be made responsible as well. Of course, the corporation must become liable for the loans. Otherwise, the corporation will be making payments on your personal debt. Obviously, the corporation can't do this, because the IRS would consider these payments as taxable income to you.

Other Contracts

Since there are many contracts involved in operating a business, it will be easy to overlook some. Contracts entered into by you will not be enforceable by the corporation, and this could cause problems. Some contracts, like insurance policies, may be changed by transferring the policy to the corporation and having the corporation formally adopt it. Other contracts, like leases or employment agreements should be formally rewritten and entered into by the corporation. This will make enforcing these contracts easier for the corporation, while reducing some of your personal liability exposure. While the incorporation of an existing business includes many variables, I hope that this short discussion on the subject has been helpful to you.

What About Partnership Agreements?

A partnership agreement is a special contract entered into by the partners of a business that is organized as a partnership. (See Chapter 3.) A partnership agreement is used to outline the basic "rules" by which the partnership will operate. All partners are bound by this agreement. The following list outlines some, but not all of the items covered in a typical partnership agreement:

- Who "owns" the business and how much of the business each partner owns

- How income and expenses will be split between the partners

- What happens to business assets if the partnership splits up

- Who will manage the business

- Who takes care of the money

- Whether one partner can sign contracts without the other's approval

- Salaries and other compensation

- The length of time for which the partnership will exist

- The purpose of the partnership

If you are currently operating your business as a partnership and want to incorporate, you'll need to do things a little differently. You see, corporations do not have "partnership" agreements. Instead, corporations have bylaws. Corporation bylaws should address most of the items listed above. After incorporating, your bylaws will determine how the business is operated. Accordingly, you should no longer use a partnership agreement if you incorporate. All of the items addressed in your current partnership agreement should be addressed by your corporation bylaws instead. Separate partnership agreements tell the IRS that you are still really operating as a partnership and you may be taxed accordingly. You don't want this to happen. If the standard bylaws included with this book do not address your specific needs, change them accordingly. To amend your bylaws:

1. Hold a directors meeting.

2. Discuss the changes needed to be made.

3. Record the changes. (Write them down)

4. Have the directors vote on the matter.

5. Record the meeting on a blank minute form found in chapter eight.

6. File the amendments with the corporate records.

5

INCORPORATION QUESTIONS

In this section, you will find many of the most commonly asked questions people have about incorporating. When I wrote my first book, *Incorporating in Tennessee Without A Lawyer*, it was about half the size of this book. Needless to say, it didn't include nearly as much information. Accordingly, my office received a lot of questions from readers. The answers to many of these questions have been included throughout this book. However, some questions can be answered in a few sentences, and don't require a whole chapter. These questions are found on the next few pages.

What are the Articles of Incorporation?
The articles of incorporation, sometimes called the certificate of incorporation, or charter, declares the desire of an individual or group of individuals to become a corporation. It spells out certain minimum information about the corporation that is required by the laws of the state. It may also contain specific information about the corporation that needs to be made public record, items like restriction on the transfer of corporate stock.

What is an Assumed Name?
An assumed name, sometimes called a fictitious name, is a feature of some state corporation laws that allows a corporation to operate under more than one name. For the details on the mechanics of this option, ask the state corporations division. This can be quite convenient to the small business person who sells different products but does not wish to have several corporations. Many people initially name the corporation their last name like Jones, Inc. They might then name their different companies to be more descriptive of separate product lines, like Quantum Computers, Inc., and Standard Computer Software Corporation. All of these

would simply be different names, or aliases for the same corporation, that has only one set of books, and the same shareholders.

What are Authorized Shares?

State law specifies that shares of stock in the corporation will be issued under the direction of the board of directors. But, since the corporation is set up to benefit the shareholders, the shareholders set, or limit, the number of shares the directors are "authorized", or allowed, to issue. Since the directors are not allowed to issue shares without authorization from the shareholders, the number of authorized shares is equal to the number of total shares.

What's the Difference Between Issued and Authorized Shares?

The board of directors control the issuance of stock. Authorized shares is the total number of shares of stock that the board of directors are "authorized" to issue to shareholders. The board may issue all the shares now, or issue some now, and some later. Authorized shares become issued shares when "issued" or distributed to a stockholder. Shares that are not issued are usually called authorized but unissued shares. Unissued shares belong to the corporation and are not considered for shareholders' ownership percentages.

What is the Board of Directors?

The board of directors is the body of people specified by state law to direct and oversee the business affairs of the corporation, and is usually headed by a chairperson. The board usually meets infrequently, and hires officers to manage the day to day business operations. However, since directors of the corporation have certain immunities from lawsuits against the corporation, all important business decisions like entering long term contracts, should be approved by the corporation's board of directors.

It is important to remember to have a corporation's "directors" approve all major corporate actions. In the case of a small corporation, you must simply put on your director's hat, and put the word director after your signature. This should be done because at some point in the future someone may try to sue you personally instead of your corporation. If you, and not your "director" or "officer" has signed all corporate paperwork, it will make it easier for the person bringing suit to prove the corporation is a sham.

This is a procedure that you need to be aware of. It's called "piercing the corporate veil". In some cases, when they realize that suing your corporation will get them nothing, people will try to sue you instead. That is, they will try to avoid your personal liability protection by going through the corporation, straight to you. Piercing the corporate veil is an expression used to suggest the action of penetrating the invisible wall of protection between you and your corporation.

To lower the success rate of these attempts, you as a shareholder should not "run" your corporation. You should put on the appropriate "hat" and let your "officers" and "directors" do this for you. If you are your own officers and directors, you must simply wear your officer or director's hat when performing these official functions. It sounds silly, but you must remember that most corporation laws were drawn up for big corporations and adapted to small ones.

What are Bylaws?

Just as a city or state government has laws for its citizens, the corporation has rules for its shareholders, officers, and directors. These rules are called the by-laws. They specify things like the number of votes required to pass a matter put before the corporation, and the requirements to be met before a shareholder can sell their stock. You may want to customize the bylaws included with this kit to address your specific needs. To customize them, hold a directors meeting, write your changes or additions on a MINUTES OF DIRECTORS MEETING included with this book, and have the directors sign the form. These changes will become part of the corporate records.

What Is a C Corporation?

The IRS, not the state, classifies corporation according to how they want to be taxed. There are two types of corporations according to the IRS, either "C" corporations, named after Subchapter C of the tax code, or "S" corporations, named after Subchapter S of the tax code. C corporations, have their own tax identification number and pay their own taxes.

Just the opposite, S corporation, sometimes called small business corporation, are taxed as if they were not a corporation. Taxed like a partnership, an S corporation "passes through" its income or losses to the shareholder's personal tax return, and is not liable for Federal income taxes itself. The shareholders of an S corporation will pay personal income taxes based on the income of the S corporation, whether or not the shareholder received any of the income. Conversely, the S corporation shareholders will be able to personally enjoy any losses the corporation may have. You need to discuss this with your CPA.

What does Capitalization Mean?

Capitalization is a term that requires a knowledge of accounting to understand, and can have different meanings. With a new corporation, the term generally refers to the amount of money that a corporation has in its "kitty" when operations begin. Some states have minimum capitalization requirements to insure that corporations have a bare minimum of assets before starting operations. Since shareholders are somewhat insulated from lawsuits against a corporation, these assets provide a means to pay any potential lawsuit winners. Minimum capitalization requirements also make it a little more difficult to start a corporation, and was probably started to help to keep out the "riff raff". Today, only a few states have minimum capitalization requirements.

What is a Certificate of Incorporation?

The certificate of incorporation is what some states issue to evidence that yours is a valid corporation and has met state incorporation requirements. In some states, however, certificate of incorporation means articles of incorporation, the document that you file to incorporate your business.

What is a Charter?

The terms Charter, Certificate of Incorporation, and Articles Of Incorporation are used interchangeably.

What are Directors?

Directors are the people who oversee the affairs of the corporation according to what they think is best for it. Directors are like politicians, hand picked by the shareholders, and subject to being removed by them. In a small corporation the directors are usually the shareholders who simply put on their director's "hat" when the need arises.

What is a Dividend?

A dividend is a special payment, usually paid at the end of each quarter, and is based on the profits made by the corporation during that quarter. Dividends are usually paid in cash or additional stock to the shareholders. This is a shareholder's reward for investing in the corporation. It is much the same as interest on a loan except that the dividend is based on the income of the corporation, and may or may not be a regular payment. Also, dividends are not deductible by the corporation while interest payments are. Some owners pay themselves a small salary to minimize FICA withholding, and pay themselves a quarterly dividend instead.

What is an Incorporator?

The incorporator is simply the person that files the articles of incorporation. The incorporator's duties and title end after incorporating. The incorporator must be old enough to legally enter into contracts. If a lawyer incorporates your business, he usually acts as the incorporator, allowing him to sign the required paperwork.

What are Issued Shares?

Issued shares are easily confused with authorized shares. Authorized shares is the maximum number of shares that the board of directors is "authorized", or allowed to issue. Issued shares, however, is the number of shares actually "issued", or given out to shareholders. Only issued shares are counted for ownership purposes.

How Many Shares of Stock are Required?

A corporation can't be a corporation without at least one share of stock. So you must have at least one shareholder, and one share of stock. You can have (authorize) as many shares of stock as you want, however, this may increase your filing fees in some cases.

What is Par Value?

Par value is simply an accounting or bookkeeping unit of measure used to keep track of the amounts given to the corporation when stock is issued. Par value means much the same as purchase price. If the stock has a $1000 par value, then the person wishing to purchase the stock must give something with at least a $1000 value for the stock. Amounts given for the stock in excess of par value are called "paid in capital in excess of par value" and again is simply a bookkeeping title. Par value is only meaningful when the stock is bought directly from the corporation and is not considered when stock is bought on the open market. When one buys stock on the market, they pay what the stock is actually worth, the "market" price.

What is no Par Value Stock?

Since par value more or less means the price to be paid for the shares when purchased from the corporation, no par value stock is stock for which no fixed price is set. This is usually the case in small corporations where the owners issue themselves a number of shares and simply infuse money in the corporation when needed. Corporations issue no par stock for flexibility. If the corporation's stock has no par value, then there is no set "price" for the stock. In this case, the directors can raise the "price" of the stock when the corporation becomes more valuable. You see, with no par value stock, the directors decide how much must be paid for the stock each time it is issued to a shareholder.

Must Stock Have a Par Value?

No. Most often in a small business corporation the stock is called "no par value stock" which simply means that there is no set amount of payment required to purchase the stock of the corporation. Each time stock is issued, the directors will decide how much must be received for the shares.

What are Officers?

The officers are usually employees of the corporation and manage the business on a daily basis. They are responsible for duties outlined by the corporate bylaws. In a small corporation, the officers are usually the directors and the shareholders, who merely "wear different hats". The owners of a small corporation do a lot of role playing because small corporations don't exactly fit the corporate mold envisioned by the laws of many states. The president is usually the chairperson of the board as well.

What is a Registered Agent?

Although a corporation is a separate legal entity, it cannot physically receive documents, and therefore needs a real person to receive them on its behalf. A registered agent is needed is to make sure that the corporation will have an assigned representative at a known address in the state to receive all legal documents for the corporation. The registered agent will forward these documents to the corporation at its principal office address. Corporations that operate in different states, but don't maintain offices in these states, use agent service companies to act as registered agent for them. Many of our out-of-state readers appoint Consumer Publishing as their registered agent in Tennessee. We charge less than half what other companies charge. The terms registered agent, resident agent, and statutory agent all have the same meaning.

What is an Annual Meeting?

The annual meeting is a special meeting held once a year to "review the results of corporate operations" with the shareholders. In larger corporations, shareholders do not generally participate in daily business operations. So, in order to make sure that shareholders are informed about their investment, corporations are required by most state laws to hold annual meetings for this purpose.

Since officers and directors are usually appointed for terms of one year, annual meetings are also held to reappoint the officers and directors of the corporation. Although holding an annual meeting may sound complicated, the requirement of holding an annual meeting is usually satisfied by using a standard pre-written form called *Minutes of Annual Shareholders Meeting* included in chapter eight. If you read through the form, you'll see that it records that the actions described above are performed.

What are Stockholders or Shareholders?

The term stockholders and shareholders are usually used interchangeably, and are the people for whom the corporation was organized. In large corporations, shareholders are merely investors who put money into the business in return for future dividends. In a small corporation, they are the people who actually start and run the corporation providing jobs for themselves.

6

S CORPORATION ELECTION

This chapter begins the second part of this book. In the next four chapters, we'll cover the subjects you'll need to consider *after* you've finished incorporating.

What is an S Corporation?

This chapter will cover the subject of S corporations, what they are, and how to form one. Before we proceed, let me make one thing perfectly clear. An S corporation is not a special kind of corporation. It is simply a corporation that elects special tax treatment allowed under Subchapter S of the Internal Revenue Tax Code. *Being an S corporation is a tax matter only.*

When you complete the formation of your corporation by following the steps outlined in this book, a new taxpaying entity will exist. The Internal Revenue Service and your state department of revenue will expect to receive taxes on the income of your new corporation. It's almost as if you had a newborn baby and the baby was expected to start paying taxes immediately. Although you can't avoid paying taxes, the IRS does give you an option that may lower them—electing to be treated as an S corporation.

Just as individuals may choose to file as either "Single", "Married", "Head of household" etc., corporations have similar filing options. A corporation may choose to file as either a "C" corporation, or an "S" corporation. If a corporation chooses to be a C corporation, it will be taxed according to Subchapter C of the IRS tax code. If a corporation chooses to be an S corporation, it will be taxed according to Subchapter S of the IRS tax code.

All new corporations are classified by the IRS as C corporations. You don't have to do anything to be a C corporation. But, if you think that filing as an S corporation will lower your taxes, you must elect to be treated as an S corporation and then notify the IRS of your choice. Notifying the IRS is a simple procedure that is accomplished by filing a single form with them—form 2553.

To be treated as an S corporation, you may also have to file a form with your state. To see if you do, contact your state department of revenue. Please remember that time limits exist regarding the filing of S corporation forms. Filing a form late may exclude you from electing S corporation status.

Prior to filing the form 2553 with the IRS and perhaps a similar form with your state department of revenue, you'll need to get director and shareholder approval to make the S corporation election. Director approval can be granted in a meeting of the directors. Their approval will be noted in the minutes of the meeting. A pre written form for your use is in this chapter. Do not send this form to the IRS. This form is for your records only. Keep it in your corporate records book.

Shareholder approval is recorded on form 2553. All you need to do is simply record the information for each shareholder and have them sign and date the form. Be sure to keep a copy of this form in your corporate record book. Send the original with original signatures to the IRS via certified mail. Technically, election of S corporation status is subject to IRS approval. Accordingly, you will receive notification by mail.

If you live in a community property state or own the shares of stock jointly with another person, then both people will be listed as shareholders and both will sign the form. Each person will show that they own half the number of shares jointly owned. For example, if a husband owns stock in a corporation and lives in a community property state, his wife legally owns half of the stock. So, both names, SSN's, and signatures will appear on the form. The number of shares that he owns will be divided in half for the purpose of completing the form. Half the number of shares will appear next to his name and half will appear next to hers.

Before we discuss the differences between S and C corporations, let's review the qualifications that your corporation must meet in order to elect S corporation status. For further details, you may want to refer to the instructions to the form. To elect S corporation status your corporation must meet all of these requirements:

1.   It must be a domestic corporation formed in the U.S.A.
2.   It may have no more than 35 shareholders.
3.   It may only have individuals, estates or certain trusts as shareholders.
4.   It may not have nonresident alien shareholders.
5.   It may only have one class of stock.
6.   It may not be an ineligible corporation. See the instructions for form 2553.

Now that you know what an S corporation is and how to elect S corporation status, lets discuss the differences between S and C corporations and which filing status may be best for your corporation. As you review this material please remember one thing. Everyone's personal tax situation is different. Although I wish I could, I can't address the specific needs of every reader. I can only discuss what works best for most people. If you feel your tax situation needs closer review, you may want to discuss it with your tax advisor.

Which is best, an S corporation or a C corporation? I've been asked this question at least a thousand times and here's my answer. It depends on your personal tax situation but, here's my opinion. Newer corporations that have net losses should be S corporation and more mature corporations that are making profits should be C corporations.

The major difference between a regular, or "C" corporation, and the small business or "S" corporation, is that a C corporation is responsible for its own income tax, while the S corporation is not liable for Federal income tax. The S corporation taxes, if any, are paid by its stockholders on their personal returns. You might say this sounds like a bad deal until you consider that many S corporations lose money, or are made to lose money, in which case the stockholder gets a deduction on his personal return.

If you own stock in a C corporation and it loses money, the loss would be the corporation's and it would not lower your personal tax bill. Conversely, if the C corporation did not pay any dividends, you would have no personal tax liability from the corporation's income. As you can see, this can be a perplexing question, the answer to which depends on your particular financial situation.

Since many chapters could be devoted to this subject, a separate subject from this manual, I will simply suggest that you discuss it with your CPA, or financial advisor. However, I will add that most corporations with less than 15 stockholders are S corporations. I will also add that since new businesses usually lose money in the first year or two, it might be advantageous to begin as an S corporation in order to pass the losses to your personal tax return. Later, when the corporation starts to make a profit, it may be advisable to terminate your S corporation Status and begin filing as a C corporation in order to let the corporation pay its own taxes.

Completing the Form
Completing the IRS form 2553 is not difficult. The only hard part is remembering to file it before you run out of time. You see, the form must be filed before the 16th day of the third month of the tax year to be effective for your first year in business. If you miss this deadline, your S corporation election won't be good until next year. Does that mean that a corporation formed June 1st is out of luck? Well, the instructions would make you to think so, but it's not the case. You see,

the tax year of a corporation formed June 1st doesn't begin until June 1. This makes August 15th the deadline for filing. My advice—file the form when you get incorporated and send it via Certified Mail. Please see the instructions for the address. Although you should read form 2553 instructions, here is a brief explanation of how to complete the form.

PART I:

Put the corporation's name, address, city and state in the space provided.

Box A.	Put your employer ID number or "applied for".
Box B.	The date your articles are filed with the state.
Box C.	The state of incorporation.
Box D.	Same as Box H. This date starts your filing time limit of 75 days.
Box E.&F.	Put your name, title, area code and phone number here.
Box G.	Check this box if your address has changed since applying for your employer tax ID number. (Form SS-4)
Box H.	The date of your organizational meeting when stock was issued.
Box I.	Put "December 31" unless your tax advisor suggests otherwise.
Box J.	List shareholder's names including joint and community property owners.
Box K.	Have each shareholder sign and date here—including spouses in community property states.
Box L.	Enter the number of shares each person has and the issue date. Joint owners and community property owners will list half of the total owned.
Box M.	Enter SSN if shareholder is an individual.
Box N.	All should be "December 31", or 12/31. Sign and date the bottom front of the form.

PART II:

Do not complete this section unless you want the tax year of your corporation to be something other than January 1 - December 31. Most people will not complete this section.

PART III:

This part is for trusts that own stock in a corporation. This section won't apply to you unless the stock of your corporation is held by a trust that you have created.

When you're finished, send the form to the same IRS office where you mail your personal tax return—listed in the instructions to the form. *If you have any questions, call the IRS at 1-800-829-1040.*

Form **2553**	**Election by a Small Business Corporation**	OMB No. 1545-0146

Form **2553**
(Rev. September 1993)
Department of the Treasury
Internal Revenue Service

Election by a Small Business Corporation
(Under section 1362 of the Internal Revenue Code)
▶ For Paperwork Reduction Act Notice, see page 1 of instructions.
▶ See separate instructions.

OMB No. 1545-0146
Expires 8-31-96

Notes: 1. *This election, to be an "S corporation," can be accepted only if all the tests are met under **Who May Elect** on page 1 of the instructions; all signatures in Parts I and III are originals (no photocopies); and the exact name and address of the corporation and other required form information are provided.*

2. *Do not file **Form 1120S**, U.S. Income Tax Return for an S Corporation, until you are notified that your election is accepted.*

Part I   Election Information

Please Type or Print

Name of corporation (see instructions)	A Employer identification number (EIN)
Number, street, and room or suite no. (If a P.O. box, see instructions.)	B Date incorporated
City or town, state, and ZIP code	C State of incorporation

D Election is to be effective for tax year beginning (month, day, year) . . . . ▶   /   /

E Name and title of officer or legal representative who the IRS may call for more information

F Telephone number of officer or legal representative
(   )

G If the corporation changed its name or address after applying for the EIN shown in **A,** check this box . . . . ▶ ☐

H If this election takes effect for the first tax year the corporation exists, enter month, day, and year of the **earliest** of the following: (1) date the corporation first had shareholders, (2) date the corporation first had assets, or (3) date the corporation began doing business . . . . ▶   /   /

I Selected tax year: Annual return will be filed for tax year ending (month and day) ▶ ....

If the tax year ends on any date other than December 31, except for an automatic 52-53-week tax year ending with reference to the month of December, you **must** complete Part II on the back. If the date you enter is the ending date of an automatic 52-53-week tax year, write "52-53-week year" to the right of the date. See Temporary Regulations section 1.441-2T(e)(3).

J Name and address of each shareholder, shareholder's spouse having a community property interest in the corporation's stock, and each tenant in common, joint tenant, and tenant by the entirety. (A husband and wife (and their estates) are counted as one shareholder in determining the number of shareholders without regard to the manner in which the stock is owned.)	K Shareholders' Consent Statement. Under penalties of perjury, we declare that we consent to the election of the above-named corporation to be an "S corporation" under section 1362(a) and that we have examined this consent statement, including accompanying schedules and statements, and to the best of our knowledge and belief, it is true, correct, and complete. (Shareholders sign and date below.)*		L Stock owned		M Social security number or employer identification number (see instructions)	N Share-holder's tax year ends (month and day)
	Signature	Date	Number of shares	Dates acquired		

*For this election to be valid, the consent of each shareholder, shareholder's spouse having a community property interest in the corporation's stock, and each tenant in common, joint tenant, and tenant by the entirety must either appear above or be attached to this form. (See instructions for Column K if a continuation sheet or a separate consent statement is needed.)

Under penalties of perjury, I declare that I have examined this election, including accompanying schedules and statements, and to the best of my knowledge and belief, it is true, correct, and complete.

Signature of officer ▶   Title ▶   Date ▶

See Parts II and III on back.   Cat. No. 18629R   Form **2553** (Rev. 9-93)

Part II **Selection of Fiscal Tax Year (All corporations using this part must complete item O and one of items P, Q, or R.)**

O Check the applicable box below to indicate whether the corporation is:

  1. ☐ A new corporation adopting the tax year entered in item I, Part I.

  2. ☐ An existing corporation retaining the tax year entered in item I, Part I.

  3. ☐ An existing corporation changing to the tax year entered in item I, Part I.

P Complete item P if the corporation is using the expeditious approval provisions of Revenue Procedure 87-32, 1987-2 C.B. 396, to request: **(1)** a natural business year (as defined in section 4.01(1) of Rev. Proc. 87-32), or **(2)** a year that satisfies the ownership tax year test in section 4.01(2) of Rev. Proc. 87-32. Check the applicable box below to indicate the representation statement the corporation is making as required under section 4 of Rev. Proc. 87-32.

  1. Natural Business Year ▶ ☐ I represent that the corporation is retaining or changing to a tax year that coincides with its natural business year as defined in section 4.01(1) of Rev. Proc. 87-32 and as verified by its satisfaction of the requirements of section 4.02(1) of Rev. Proc. 87-32. In addition, if the corporation is changing to a natural business year as defined in section 4.01(1), I further represent that such tax year results in less deferral of income to the owners than the corporation's present tax year. I also represent that the corporation is not described in section 3.01(2) of Rev. Proc. 87-32. (See instructions for additional information that must be attached.)

  2. Ownership Tax Year ▶ ☐ I represent that shareholders holding more than half of the shares of the stock (as of the first day of the tax year to which the request relates) of the corporation have the same tax year or are concurrently changing to the tax year that the corporation adopts, retains, or changes to per item I, Part I. I also represent that the corporation is not described in section 3.01(2) of Rev. Proc. 87-32.

Note: *If you do not use item P and the corporation wants a fiscal tax year, complete either item Q or R below. Item Q is used to request a fiscal tax year based on a business purpose and to make a back-up section 444 election. Item R is used to make a regular section 444 election.*

Q Business Purpose—To request a fiscal tax year based on a business purpose, you must check box Q1 and pay a user fee. See instructions for details. You may also check box Q2 and/or box Q3.

  1. Check here ▶ ☐ if the fiscal year entered in item I, Part I, is requested under the provisions of section 6.03 of Rev. Proc. 87-32. Attach to Form 2553 a statement showing the business purpose for the requested fiscal year. See instructions for additional information that must be attached.

  2. Check here ▶ ☐ to show that the corporation intends to make a back-up section 444 election in the event the corporation's business purpose request is not approved by the IRS. (See instructions for more information.)

  3. Check here ▶ ☐ to show that the corporation agrees to adopt or change to a tax year ending December 31 if necessary for the IRS to accept this election for S corporation status in the event: (1) the corporation's business purpose request is not approved and the corporation makes a back-up section 444 election, but is ultimately not qualified to make a section 444 election, or (2) the corporation's business purpose request is not approved and the corporation did not make a back-up section 444 election.

R Section 444 Election—To make a section 444 election, you must check box R1 and you may also check box R2.

  1. Check here ▶ ☐ to show the corporation will make, if qualified, a section 444 election to have the fiscal tax year shown in item I, Part I. To make the election, you must complete **Form 8716,** Election To Have a Tax Year Other Than a Required Tax Year, and either attach it to Form 2553 or file it separately.

  2. Check here ▶ ☐ to show that the corporation agrees to adopt or change to a tax year ending December 31 if necessary for the IRS to accept this election for S corporation status in the event the corporation is ultimately not qualified to make a section 444 election.

Part III **Qualified Subchapter S Trust (QSST) Election Under Section 1361(d)(2)****

Income beneficiary's name and address	Social security number
Trust's name and address	Employer identification number

Date on which stock of the corporation was transferred to the trust (month, day, year) . . . . ▶   /   /

In order for the trust named above to be a QSST and thus a qualifying shareholder of the S corporation for which this Form 2553 is filed, I hereby make the election under section 1361(d)(2). Under penalties of perjury, I certify that the trust meets the definitional requirements of section 1361(d)(3) and that all other information provided in Part III is true, correct, and complete.

_____   _____
Signature of income beneficiary or signature and title of legal representative or other qualified person making the election   Date

**Use of Part III to make the QSST election may be made only if stock of the corporation has been transferred to the trust on or before the date on which the corporation makes its election to be an S corporation. The QSST election must be made and filed separately if stock of the corporation is transferred to the trust after the date on which the corporation makes the S election.

Department of the Treasury
Internal Revenue Service

Instructions for Form 2553
(Revised September 1993)

Election by a Small Business Corporation

Section references are to the Internal Revenue Code unless otherwise noted.

Paperwork Reduction Act Notice.—We ask for the information on this form to carry out the Internal Revenue laws of the United States. You are required to give us the information. We need it to ensure that you are complying with these laws and to allow us to figure and collect the right amount of tax.

The time needed to complete and file this form will vary depending on individual circumstances. The estimated average time is:

Recordkeeping	6 hr., 13 min.
Learning about the law or the form	2 hr., 59 min.
Preparing, copying, assembling, and sending the form to the IRS	3 hr., 13 min.

If you have comments concerning the accuracy of these time estimates or suggestions for making this form more simple, we would be happy to hear from you. You can write to both the **Internal Revenue Service,** Attention: Reports Clearance Officer, T:FP, Washington, DC 20224; and the **Office of Management and Budget,** Paperwork Reduction Project (1545-0146), Washington, DC 20503. **DO NOT** send the tax form to either of these offices. Instead, see **Where To File** below.

General Instructions

Purpose.—To elect to be an "S corporation," a corporation must file Form 2553. The election permits the income of the S corporation to be taxed to the shareholders of the corporation rather than to the corporation itself, except as provided in Subchapter S of the Code. For more information, get **Pub. 589,** Tax Information on S Corporations.

Who May Elect.—A corporation may elect to be an S corporation only if it meets **all** of the following tests:

1. It is a domestic corporation.

2. It has no more than 35 shareholders. A husband and wife (and their estates) are treated as one shareholder for this requirement. All other persons are treated as separate shareholders.

3. It has only individuals, estates, or certain trusts as shareholders. See the instructions for Part III regarding qualified subchapter S trusts.

4. It has no nonresident alien shareholders.

5. It has only one class of stock (disregarding differences in voting rights). Generally, a corporation is treated as having only one class of stock if all outstanding shares of the corporation's stock confer identical rights to distribution and liquidation

proceeds. See Regulations section 1.1361-1(l) for more details.

6. It is not one of the following ineligible corporations:

a. A corporation that owns 80% or more of the stock of another corporation, unless the other corporation has not begun business and has no gross income;

b. A bank or thrift institution;

c. An insurance company subject to tax under the special rules of Subchapter L of the Code;

d. A corporation that has elected to be treated as a possessions corporation under section 936; or

e. A domestic international sales corporation (DISC) or former DISC.

7. It has a permitted tax year as required by section 1378 or makes a section 444 election to have a tax year other than a permitted tax year. Section 1378 defines a permitted tax year as a tax year ending December 31, or any other tax year for which the corporation establishes a business purpose to the satisfaction of the IRS. See Part II for details on requesting a fiscal tax year based on a business purpose or on making a section 444 election.

8. Each shareholder consents as explained in the instructions for Column K.

See sections 1361, 1362, and 1378 for additional information on the above tests.

Where To File.—File this election with the Internal Revenue Service Center listed below.

If the corporation's principal business, office, or agency is located in ▼	Use the following Internal Revenue Service Center address ▼
New Jersey, New York (New York City and counties of Nassau, Rockland, Suffolk, and Westchester)	Holtsville, NY 00501
New York (all other counties), Connecticut, Maine, Massachusetts, New Hampshire, Rhode Island, Vermont	Andover, MA 05501
Illinois, Iowa, Minnesota, Missouri, Wisconsin	Kansas City, MO 64999
Delaware, District of Columbia, Maryland, Pennsylvania, Virginia	Philadelphia, PA 19255
Florida, Georgia, South Carolina	Atlanta, GA 39901
Indiana, Kentucky, Michigan, Ohio, West Virginia	Cincinnati, OH 45999
Kansas, New Mexico, Oklahoma, Texas	Austin, TX 73301
Alaska, Arizona, California (counties of Alpine, Amador, Butte, Calaveras, Colusa, Contra Costa, Del Norte, El Dorado, Glenn, Humboldt, Lake, Lassen, Marin, Mendocino, Modoc, Napa, Nevada, Placer, Plumas, Sacramento, San Joaquin, Shasta, Sierra, Siskiyou, Solano, Sonoma, Sutter, Tehama, Trinity, Yolo, and Yuba), Colorado, Idaho, Montana, Nebraska, Nevada, North Dakota, Oregon, South Dakota, Utah, Washington, Wyoming	Ogden, UT 84201
California (all other counties), Hawaii	Fresno, CA 93888
Alabama, Arkansas, Louisiana, Mississippi, North Carolina, Tennessee	Memphis, TN 37501

When To Make the Election.—Complete and file Form 2553 **(a)** at any time before the 16th day of the third month of the tax year, if filed during the tax year the election is to take effect, or **(b)** at any time during the preceding tax year. An election made no later than 2 months and 15 days after the beginning of a tax year that is less than 2½ months long is treated as timely made for that tax year. An election made after the 15th day of the third month but before the end of the tax year is effective for the next year. For example, if a calendar tax year corporation makes the election in April 1994, it is effective for the corporation's 1995 calendar tax year. See section 1362(b) for more information.

Acceptance or Nonacceptance of Election.—The Service Center will notify the corporation if its election is accepted and when it will take effect. The corporation will also be notified if its election is not accepted. The corporation should generally receive a determination on its election within 60 days after it has filed Form 2553. If box Q1 in Part II is checked on page 2, the corporation will receive a ruling letter from the IRS in Washington, DC, that either approves or denies the selected tax year. When box Q1 is checked, it will generally take an additional 90 days for the Form 2553 to be accepted.

Do not file Form 1120S until the corporation is notified that its election has been accepted. If the corporation is now required to file **Form 1120,** U.S. Corporation Income Tax Return, or any other applicable tax return, continue filing it until the election takes effect.

Care should be exercised to ensure that the IRS receives the election. If the corporation is not notified of acceptance or nonacceptance of its election within 3 months

Cat. No. 49978N

of date of filing (date mailed), or within 6 months if box Q1 is checked, please take follow-up action by corresponding with the Service Center where the corporation filed the election. If the IRS questions whether Form 2553 was filed, an acceptable proof of filing is: (a) certified or registered mail receipt (timely filed); (b) Form 2553 with accepted stamp; (c) Form 2553 with stamped IRS received date; or (d) IRS letter stating that Form 2553 has been accepted.

End of Election.— Once the election is made, it stays in effect for all years until it is terminated. During the 5 years after the election is terminated under section 1362(d), the corporation (or a successor corporation) can make another election on Form 2553 only with IRS consent. See Regulations section 1.1362-5 for more details.

Specific Instructions

Part I

Part I must be completed by all corporations.

Name and Address of Corporation.—Enter the true corporate name as set forth in the corporate charter or other legal document creating it. If the corporation's mailing address is the same as someone else's, such as a shareholder's, please enter "c/o" and this person's name following the name of the corporation. Include the suite, room, or other unit number after the street address. If the Post Office does not deliver to the street address and the corporation has a P.O. box, show the box number instead of the street address. If the corporation changed its name or address after applying for its EIN, be sure to check the box in item G of Part I.

Item A. Employer Identification Number.—If the corporation has applied for an employer identification number (EIN) but has not received it, enter "applied for." If the corporation does not have an EIN, it should apply for one on **Form SS-4,** Application for Employer Identification Number, available from most IRS and Social Security Administration offices.

Item D. Effective Date of Election.—Enter the beginning effective date (month, day, year) of the tax year requested for the S corporation. Generally, this will be the beginning effective date of the tax year for which the ending effective date is required to be shown in item I, Part I. For a new corporation (first year the corporation exists) it will generally be the date required to be shown in item H, Part I. The tax year of a new corporation starts on the date that it has shareholders, acquires assets, or begins doing business, whichever happens first. If the effective date for item D for a newly formed corporation is later than the date in item H, the corporation should file Form 1120 or Form 1120-A, for the tax period between these dates.

Column K. Shareholders' Consent Statement.—Each shareholder who owns (or is deemed to own) stock at the time the election is made must consent to the election. If the election is made during the corporation's tax year for which it first takes effect, any person who held stock at any time during the part of that year that occurs before the election is made, must consent to the election, even though the person may have sold or transferred his or her stock before the

election is made. Each shareholder consents by signing and dating in column K or signing and dating a separate consent statement described below.

An election made during the first 2½ months of the tax year is effective for the following tax year if any person who held stock in the corporation during the part of the tax year before the election was made, and who did not hold stock at the time the election was made, did not consent to the election.

If a husband and wife have a community interest in the stock or in the income from it, both must consent. Each tenant in common, joint tenant, and tenant by the entirety also must consent.

A minor's consent is made by the minor or the legal representative of the minor, or by a natural or adoptive parent of the minor if no legal representative has been appointed.

The consent of an estate is made by an executor or administrator.

If stock is owned by a trust that is a qualified shareholder, the deemed owner of the trust must consent. See section 1361(c)(2) for details regarding qualified trusts that may be shareholders and rules on determining who is the deemed owner of the trust.

Continuation sheet or separate consent statement.—If you need a continuation sheet or use a separate consent statement, attach it to Form 2553. The separate consent statement must contain the name, address, and employer identification number of the corporation and the shareholder information requested in columns J through N of Part I.

If you want, you may combine all the shareholders' consents in one statement.

Column L.—Enter the number of shares of stock each shareholder owns and the dates the stock was acquired. If the election is made during the corporation's tax year for which it first takes effect, do not list the shares of stock for those shareholders who sold or transferred all of their stock before the election was made. However, these shareholders must still consent to the election for it to be effective for the tax year.

Column M.—Enter the social security number of each shareholder who is an individual. Enter the employer identification number of each shareholder that is an estate or a qualified trust.

Column N.—Enter the month and day that each shareholder's tax year ends. If a shareholder is changing his or her tax year, enter the tax year the shareholder is changing to, and attach an explanation indicating the present tax year and the basis for the change (e.g., automatic revenue procedure or letter ruling request).

If the election is made during the corporation's tax year for which it first takes effect, you do not have to enter the tax year of any shareholder who sold or transferred all of his or her stock before the election was made.

Signature.—Form 2553 must be signed by the president, treasurer, assistant treasurer, chief accounting officer, or other corporate officer (such as tax officer) authorized to sign.

Part II

Complete Part II if you selected a tax year ending on any date other than December 31

(other than a 52-53-week tax year ending with reference to the month of December).

Box P1.—Attach a statement showing separately for each month the amount of gross receipts for the most recent 47 months as required by section 4.03(3) of Revenue Procedure 87-32, 1987-2 C.B. 396. A corporation that does not have a 47-month period of gross receipts cannot establish a natural business year under section 4.01(1).

Box Q1.—For examples of an acceptable business purpose for requesting a fiscal tax year, see Revenue Ruling 87-57, 1987-2 C.B. 117.

In addition to a statement showing the business purpose for the requested fiscal year, you must attach the other information necessary to meet the ruling request requirements of Revenue Procedure 93-1, 1993-1 I.R.B. 10 (updated annually). Also attach a statement that shows separately the amount of gross receipts from sales or services (and inventory costs, if applicable) for each of the 36 months preceding the effective date of the election to be an S corporation. If the corporation has been in existence for fewer than 36 months, submit figures for the period of existence.

If you check box Q1, you must also pay a user fee of $200 (subject to change). Do not pay the fee when filing Form 2553. The Service Center will send Form 2553 to the IRS in Washington, DC, who, in turn, will notify the corporation that the fee is due. See Revenue Procedure 93-23, 1993-19 I.R.B. 6.

Box Q2.—If the corporation makes a back-up section 444 election for which it is qualified, then the election must be exercised in the event the business purpose request is not approved. Under certain circumstances, the tax year requested under the back-up section 444 election may be different than the tax year requested under business purpose. See **Form 8716,** Election To Have a Tax Year Other Than a Required Tax Year, for details on making a back-up section 444 election.

Boxes Q2 and R2.—If the corporation is not qualified to make the section 444 election after making the item Q2 back-up section 444 election or indicating its intention to make the election in item R1, and therefore it later files a calendar year return, it should write "Section 444 Election Not Made" in the top left corner of the 1st calendar year Form 1120S it files.

Part III

Certain Qualified Subchapter S Trusts (QSSTs) may make the QSST election required by section 1361(d)(2) in Part III. Part III may be used to make the QSST election only if corporate stock has been transferred to the trust on or before the date on which the corporation makes its election to be an S corporation. However, a statement can be used in lieu of Part III to make the election.

Note: *Part III may be used only in conjunction with making the Part I election (i.e., Form 2553 cannot be filed with only Part III completed).*

The deemed owner of the QSST must also consent to the S corporation election in column K, page 1, of Form 2553. See section 1361(c)(2).

*U.S. Government Printing Office: 1993 — 301-628/80221

MINUTES OF A SPECIAL MEETING OF THE BOARD OF DIRECTORS
OF

_____

Pursuant to the laws of the state in which this corporation is organized, and its bylaws, a meeting of the Directors of the above named Corporation was held at the offices of the corporation. The meeting was held on the _____ day of _____ at _____ o'clock PM/am. Present at the meeting was a quorum of directors, and all have signed their names below. As evidenced by their signatures, the directors hereby waive any meeting notice that may be required. The meeting was duly called to order and the following items of business were resolved.

1. It is decided that in the best interest of the stockholders the Corporation should elect federal taxation treatment under Subchapter S of the Internal Revenue Code as provided by the Internal Revenue Service, which would allow the Corporation to be taxed as a partnership, with the income or loss of the Corporation "passing through" to the stockholders. Consent and agreement of the stockholders will be evidenced by their signatures on Federal Tax Form Number 2553, a copy of which shall be included in the records of the Corporation. By electing tax treatment under Subchapter S, the Corporation will be required to use a calendar year with the tax year ending December 31, of each year.

2. All directors hereby approve of the action.

Having concluded all current business, the meeting was duly concluded.

_____   _____
Director   President

_____   _____
Director   Secretary

_____   _____
Director   Date

_____
Director

7

CORPORATION BYLAWS

The bylaws of the corporation are the rules by which it operates. Just as a city has laws for its citizens, a corporation has laws for its shareholders, directors, and officers. The only thing you'll need to do with the bylaws is read them, and become familiar with your corporate rules. Become especially familiar with the procedure a shareholder must follow before selling any stock as outlined in article four.

Also, note in article five you must complete the time and date of the annual meeting of the corporation. This can be any date and time that is convenient for you that allows enough time to prepare financial reports for the year just ended. It is important that you hold an annual meeting or at least sign the pre-written minutes because the directors and officers are only appointed for one year terms and are reappointed every year at this time. Remember, the minutes of the annual shareholders meeting have already been prepared, so all you really need to do is sign and date them. Most people never really have an annual shareholder's meeting, they just sign the minutes and file them away.

Since these Bylaws are standard and written for most corporations, you may feel the need to customize or add to the Bylaws. You may do this by holding a meeting, and writing the changes on a blank *Minutes of Directors Meeting* included in the next section.

This discussion is concluded on the next page.

You may want to customize your bylaws in these areas:

- Dividends - when and how much will be paid.

- Officer salaries.

- Directors compensation - if, when, and how much will be paid.

- Further conditions for the transfer of stock, like what to do in the event of the death of a shareholder. Will the stock be left to the spouse, or must it be sold back to the corporation?

- What happens if the corporation dissolves. How will the assets be distributed?

- At some point in the future a shareholder may want to leave the corporation and sell his stock. How do you determine what the stock is worth? It's better to determine this in advance to prevent arguments. Many corporations value stock by taking the stockholder's equity (Assets - Liabilities) and dividing it by the number of shares. Other corporations have director meetings about once every six months to set a value for the shares. The method is up to you.

BYLAWS
OF

_____

The following shall be known as the bylaws of the Corporation, the bylaws being rules of self government of the Corporation. These bylaws are the set of rules by which the Corporation operates on a daily basis and settles disputes that may arise from time to time; and they are binding on all those associated with the Corporation either now, or in the future. If the Bylaws are found to be inconsistent with State Law, then State Law will override. The Bylaws may be amended by the Directors provided there is a majority of Directors votes favoring the amendments.

ARTICLE ONE
PURPOSE

The Corporation may take advantage of the rights granted to it by State law, and engage in any business allowed by State Business Corporation Law.

ARTICLE TWO
DURATION

The Corporation has perpetual duration and succession in its corporate name and will exist until such time that the Board of Directors elects to end its existence.

ARTICLE THREE
POWERS

The Corporation has the powers given by State Business Corporation Law, to do all things necessary or practical to carry out its business and affairs including without limitation, the power to sue, make contracts, deal in property of any kind, make investments, borrow or lend money, be a part of another entity, or conduct its business in any way allowed by the laws of this State.

ARTICLE FOUR
SHARES

The shares of the Corporation will be common stock, with full voting rights and identical rights and privileges, with no par value. The issuance of shares will be governed by the Board of Directors, as will be the consideration to be paid for the shares, which will meet the requirements of State Business Corporation Law. The

Corporation through its Board of Directors may issue fractional shares, acquire its own shares, declare and pay cash or stock dividends, or issue certificates.

In order to insure the continued existence of the Corporation, the transfer of shares of the Corporation to any individual or other entity will be restricted in the manner described herein. No shares may be transferred on the books of the Corporation unless the number of shares are first offered to the Corporation, and then to the other shareholders on a right of first refusal basis, the corporation having first option. This option to purchase the stock will expire in thirty (30) days from when offered. If the option is not exercised within the stated period, the Shareholder may dispose of the shares in any manner he wishes. The share certificates shall bear the following notice: RESTRICTED STOCK

ARTICLE FIVE
MEETINGS

Regular Meetings

The Corporation may hold any number of meetings to conduct its business. At a minimum, it will hold an annual Shareholders' meeting at which the Directors will review with the Shareholders the operating results of the Corporation for the prior year, hold elections for Directors, and conduct any other business that may be necessary at that time. Unless decided otherwise at the time, the place and time for the annual Shareholders' meeting will be at the offices of the Corporation on the _____ day of _____ at _____ o'clock am/PM, each year. The Secretary will give proper notice to the Shareholders as may be required by law, however that notice may be waived by the Shareholder by submitting a signed waiver either before or after the meeting, or by his attendance at the meeting. Meetings may be held in or out of this State. Minutes must be taken by the Secretary for inclusion in the Corporate Records.

Special Meetings

The Corporation may hold meetings from time to time at such times and places that may be convenient. These meetings may be Directors meetings or Shareholder meetings or combined Director and Shareholder meetings. Special Shareholder meetings may be called by The Board of Directors or demanded in writing by the holders of Ten percent or more shares. Special Director meetings may be called by the Chairman, the President, or any two Directors. The Corporate Secretary will give proper notice as may be required by law, however that notice may be waived by the individual by submitting a signed waiver either before or after the meeting, or by his attendance at the meeting. Meetings may be held in or out of this State. Minutes must be taken by the Secretary for inclusion in the Corporate Records.

ARTICLE SIX
VOTING

From time to time it may be necessary for a Director or Shareholder to vote on issues brought before a meeting. No voting may take place at a meeting unless there is a quorum present. That is, a quorum of Directors must be present at a meeting before any Director may vote, and likewise a quorum of Shareholders must be present at a meeting before any Shareholder may vote. A quorum of Directors at a meeting is defined as a majority of the number of Directors. A quorum of Shareholders at a meeting is defined as a majority of the shares entitled to vote. If a quorum is present at a meeting, action on a matter may be passed if the number of votes favoring the action is cast by a majority. For voting purposes, a Director may cast one vote, and a Shareholder may cast one vote for each share held except in the case of director elections when voting is cumulative. A Shareholder may vote in person or by proxy.

ARTICLE SEVEN
ACTION WITHOUT MEETING

Directors or Shareholders may approve actions without a formal meeting if all entitled to vote on a matter consent to taking such action without a meeting. A majority still is required to pass actions without a meeting. The action must be evidenced by a written consent describing the action taken, signed by the Directors or Shareholders (depending on which group is taking the action) indicating each signer's vote or abstention on the matter, and it must be delivered to the Corporate Secretary for inclusion with the Corporate Records.

ARTICLE EIGHT
DIRECTORS

All corporate powers will be exercised by, or under the authority of, and the business affairs of the Corporation managed under the direction of, its Board of Directors. The Board may consist of one or more individuals, who need not need be Shareholders or residents of this state. The terms of the initial Directors or subsequently elected Directors will end at the next Shareholders' meeting following their election, at which time new Directors will be elected or the current Directors will be reelected.

A director may resign at any time by delivering a written notice to the Corporation. A Director may be removed at any time with or without cause if the number of votes cast to remove him exceeds the number of votes cast not to remove him. Vacancies on the Board will be filled by the Shareholders in the manner described above.

The Directors of the Corporation are not liable to either the Corporation or its Shareholders for monetary damages for a breach of fiduciary duties unless the breach involves disloyalty to the Corporation or its Shareholders, acts or omissions not in good faith, or self dealing. The Corporation may indemnify the Directors or Officers who are named as defendants in litigation relating to Corporate affairs and the Directors or Officers role therein.

ARTICLE NINE
OFFICERS

The officers of the Corporation will be initially appointed by the Board of Directors. The officers of the Corporation will be at least those required by State law, and any other officers that the Board of Directors may deem necessary. The duties and responsibilities of the Officers will be set by, and will be under the continued direction of, the Directors. Officers may be removed at any time with or without cause, and may resign at any time by delivering written notice to the Board of Directors. If allowed by state law, one person may hold more than one officer position.

PRESIDENT The President is the principal executive officer of the Corporation and in general supervises and directs the daily business operations of the Corporation, subject to the direction of the Board of Directors. The President is also the proper official to execute contracts, share certificates, and any other document that may be required on behalf of the Corporation. The President shall also preside at all meetings of Directors or meetings of Shareholders.

SECRETARY The Corporate Secretary will in general be responsible for the records of the Corporation which generally includes keeping minutes at any meeting, giving proper notice of any meeting, maintaining the Director and Shareholder registers and transfer records; and along with the President, sign stock certificates of the Corporation.

VICE PRESIDENT The Corporate Vice-President if appointed will be responsible for duties to be assigned by the Board of Directors.

TREASURER The Corporate treasurer if appointed will be responsible for duties to be assigned by the Board of Directors.

OTHER OFFICERS The directors may appoint other officers as they deem necessary.

8

RECORD KEEPING

Every list of pros and cons of incorporating I've ever seen usually lists increased record keeping at the top of the cons list. Although there is more record keeping involved with a corporation, listing increased record keeping as the top reason not to incorporate is shortsighted. Corporate record keeping is not a big deal.

To understand the reason a corporation requires more records than an unincorporated business, lets review Chapter 2 for a minute. Remember that a corporation is a separate and distinct entity with legal rights of its own that acts for or on the behalf of its shareholders. Owners incorporate their business to allow them to act through the corporation. Although the corporation is a legal "person" it cannot act for itself. So, to allow the corporation to carry out its business, the shareholders appoint directors to manage and direct the business affairs of the corporation. The directors act like the trustees of an incompetent adult, planning and directing the activities of the corporation. Since the directors are acting in a trustee type arrangement, states require that everything done by the directors on behalf on the corporation be documented. That's why every time a meeting is held to take action on behalf of the corporation, it must be documented, and minutes of the meeting must be recorded.

Another reason extensive records of corporate activities are kept is the shareholder. Remember that when corporate laws were originally drafted, the idea of a one or two person corporation had not been considered. Laws were originally drafted to match the textbook example of a corporation described in Chapter 2. In such a case, the shareholders, officers, and directors were all different people. Laws were written to protect the shareholder from unscrupulous directors and officers who would run a corporation broke to make themselves rich. This is another reason things must be documented and annual shareholders meetings held, to keep officers and directors honest by documenting their every move.

Of course, your corporation will probably be formed with less that four shareholders. These shareholders will probably be the officers, and directors as well. In this case, the shareholders will know the events within their corporation. Considering this, record keeping may seem like a waste but you must remember one thing. Operating as a corporation can give you great benefits, legally, and in the area of taxes too. To make sure that these abilities are not abused, states and the IRS require that you keep records of all corporate activities. Basically records must be kept of all important events within the corporation.

In Chapter 1, I discussed lawyers' use of a "corporate kit". This corporate kit not only includes the pre-prepared forms used to incorporate a business, but it also serves as a corporate record book, a place to keep all formal records of the corporation. These corporate record books are usually available only through lawyer supply companies, but they can be found at some office supply stores. If you want to use a formal corporate record book and cannot find one locally, you can get one through Consumer Publishing. See the brochure at the end of the book.

Below is a list of the records you must keep for your corporation. These records must be available for shareholder inspection and accordingly should be kept at the offices of the corporation in an orderly manner.

- Minutes of all shareholder and director meetings, generally for the last 3 years.
- Appropriate accounting records and financial reports.
- An alphabetical list of all shareholders with their addresses.
- An alphabetical list of all directors with their business addresses.
- An alphabetical list of all officers with their business addresses.
- Copies of all formal documents used to incorporate the business.
- All written communications to shareholders for the past 3 years.
- Financial statements for the past 3 years.
- A copy of the most recent annual report.
- All contracts entered into by the corporation.
- Amendments to, or changes in the corporate bylaws.
- Records of stock issues and transfers.
- Promissory notes.
- Life insurance policies held on corporate officers and directors.

Meetings

You will remember that the corporation is a separate "person" that cannot physically act for itself, so it acts through its directors. Whenever directors meet to discuss and decide what the corporation will do, the meeting, and what happened, must be recorded. To record your director meetings, you may use the enclosed *Minutes of Directors Meeting* sheets, or the meeting forms in your corporate records book.

The recording of meetings and even the meeting itself need not be made over formalized. For example, many people formally call the meeting to order; formally ask for turns to speak; formally make, and second motions; and formally adjourn the meeting. This formality comes from directors meetings of large corporations, and is not necessary for small corporate meetings, so don't get caught in this over structured form.

All you need to do is sit down, discuss what needs to be done, vote on the matter, write it all down on one of the minute sheets, and have everyone sign it. The best way to do this is to write down everything that happens on a plain piece of paper, summarize, and organize the information later, and then record it all on one of the minute sheets.

Blank minutes sheets for shareholder meetings are also included in this section but before using them, please note this word of caution. The only reason shareholders should meet is to discuss items of business regarding stock or the directors of the corporation. Shareholders should not discuss the day to day business of the corporation or make business decisions because of the reasons discussed in chapter two.

Please refer back to the diagram on page 20. Notice that the realm of shareholder control ends at the point where directors are chosen. Accordingly, Shareholders should only be concerned with items regarding stock and directors. These items might include things like authorizing additional shares of stock, or choosing new directors.

If you have no other meetings, you must have an annual shareholders meeting to "discuss" the results of operations for the year with the shareholders. To simplify this, enclosed is a completed *Minutes of Annual Shareholders Meeting* for your use. It contains all the wording required by State law, and all you need to do is sign the appropriate lines and date the form. Many people don't actually hold a meeting, they just sign the minutes of the meeting and file it in your corporate records binder. Before using them, make extra copies of the forms in this chapter for your future use.

MINUTES OF DIRECTORS MEETING

Pursuant to the laws of the state in which this corporation is organized, and its bylaws, a meeting of the Directors of the Corporation was held at the offices of the corporation. The meeting was held on the _____ day of _____, at _____ o'clock PM/am. Present at the meeting was a quorum of directors, and all have signed their names below. As evidenced by their signatures, the directors hereby waive any meeting notice that may be required. The meeting was duly called to order and the following items of business were resolved.

_____   _____
Director   President

_____   _____
Director   Secretary

_____   _____
Director   Date

_____
Director

MINUTES OF SHAREHOLDERS MEETING

Pursuant to the laws of the state in which this corporation is organized, and its bylaws, a meeting of the Shareholders of the Corporation was held at the offices of the corporation. The meeting was held on the _____ day of _____, at _____ o'clock PM/am. Present at the meeting was a quorum of Shareholders, and all have signed their names below. As evidenced by their signatures, the Shareholders hereby waive any meeting notice that may be required. The meeting was duly called to order and the following items of business were resolved.

_____   _____
Shareholder   President

_____   _____
Shareholder   Secretary

_____   _____
Shareholder   Date

_____
Shareholder

CHAPTER EIGHT

MINUTES OF ANNUAL SHAREHOLDERS MEETING

As required by State Law, the minutes of the annual meeting of Shareholders of the Corporation are recorded here. The meeting was held at the offices of the Corporation on the date below. Present at the meeting were the Shareholders who have signed their names below. As evidenced by their signatures, the Shareholders hereby waive any meeting notice that may be required.

After the meeting was duly called to order, it was noted that a quorum of shareholders was present, and the following items of business were conducted:

FIRST

The persons who are now Directors were elected to remain Directors until the next annual Shareholders meeting, or until they are removed or resign.

SECOND

The persons who are now Officers were elected to remain Officers until the next annual Shareholders meeting, or until they are removed or resign.

THIRD

Various items of business were discussed including the financial position of the company, and results of operations for the year just ending. Copies of the income statement and balance sheet shall be attached to these minutes.

FINALLY

Having discussed all the items to be discussed at this meeting, it was duly adjourned.

_____   _____
Shareholder   President

_____   _____
Shareholder   Secretary

_____   _____
Shareholder   Date

_____
Shareholder

9

YOUR NEW BUSINESS

Although this chapter has nothing to do with incorporating a business, working for myself has been so enjoyable, I want to do whatever I can to help you succeed. In this chapter I'll discuss a few things that will help you know what to encounter when starting a new business. This chapter is only a primer, and only covers a few basics. If you want to succeed in business, take advantage of the information presented here. Then, read other books, attend IRS seminars, and take advantage of the SBA programs offered in your area.

If you don't enjoy reading or don't have time, I'd like to share three ideas with you that work well for me and other husband and wife teams that I know. My wife loves to read, and she makes time for it. So, she reads for both of us. Together, we'll choose books that appear to offer something beneficial. She actually reads the book, and from time to time shares items of particular interest with me. If a section is particularly important, she highlights the section for me to read later. Similarly, a friend of mine who has a consulting business utilizes this team approach. His wife attends IRS and other seminars to learn how to better manage their business and their taxes. If neither you or your partner have time to read books or attend seminars, I have found that many books are available on tape. Listening to books on tape is a real time saver, and can make the difference between learning new ideas or not. Remember that knowledge is power. Knowing how to incorporate a business is powerful enough to save you several hundred dollars. Please don't let your learning process end here.

Free Help

Volumes can, and have been written about the subjects in this chapter. However, what we want to accomplish in this section is to help familiarize you with some things you may be experiencing for the first time. If you desire additional information on any of these subjects, or how to start a business in general, there are several excellent places to get free or low cost information about starting a business. Here's a list of the best:

- The U.S. Small Business Administration sponsors small business development centers (SBDCs) at community colleges in your area. These SBDCs offer FREE CONSULTING to small business owners. These offices are staffed by experienced business people and can provide invaluable help to you. To find one in your area, call the community colleges in your area and ask them if they have a small business development center on campus. If you have no luck, call your local chamber of commerce and ask them. Take advantage of this program funded by your tax dollars.

- The U.S. Small Business Administration also sponsors SCORE offices in your area. Separate from the SBDCs, these centers are staffed by retired executives in your area, and also provide free consulting. To find SCORE offices in your area, look in your telephone directory under the Federal Government listings under Small Business Administration SCORE office.

- The SBA publishes books, videos, and pamphlets at little or no cost to you. For a list of these publications, write SBA Publications, P.O. Box 30, Denver CO 80201-0030, and request a catalog.

- Your chamber of commerce is there to help local businesses. They are familiar with the requirements of local and state governments and can provide you with invaluable information that will save you a lot of time and mistakes. Call them and ask if they have any information about starting a new business.

Opening a Checking Account for a Corporation

Opening a corporate checking account is done after you finish incorporating—that is after you've done everything in chapter ten.

Opening a checking account for a corporation is basically the same as opening one for your sole proprietorship, or yourself personally, except for one thing. The bank will ask you for a corporate resolution. A corporate resolution is simply a document signed by the officers or directors of the corporation stating that you have been given authority to open a checking account for the corporation. Remember that although a corporation can have a checking account, it cannot physically go to the bank and open one. You have to do this on behalf of the corporation. The bank simply wants to make sure that the directors of the corporation have given you permission to do so. Most larger banks will have a blank corporate resolution of their own. The resolution will usually outline things like:

- The name of the corporation.

- Who has authority to open accounts on behalf of the corporation.

- Who has authority to make deposits into corporate accounts.

- Who has authority to write checks from the corporate accounts.

- How many signatures are required to sign a check for it to be valid. *(The last blank on the form.)*

In case your bank does not provide one, at the end of this chapter is a corporate resolution that you can use. You may photocopy it for your use. The bank officer will need to see you, and all those involved with the corporate checking account sign the form. So, everyone involved with the corporate checkbook needs to go to the bank when you open the checking account. Also, some readers ask if all officers, shareholders, and directors need to sign on the account. The answer is no, but if only one person can write checks on the account, and something happens to that person, the others will have a difficult time getting to the money. Accordingly, at least two people should have access to the corporate funds.

Getting a Federal Tax ID Number
Getting a Federal tax/employer ID number is done after you finish incorporating—that is after you've done everything in chapter ten.

Basically, a Federal tax ID number is a Social Security number for your business. The IRS uses a tax ID number to keep up with your business, and maintain a record of the various tax reports and returns that you are required to file, as well as your tax payments. You'll need a tax ID number if:

1. You have one or more employees (this -includes you and your spouse), or

2. If you have a pension plan, or

3. If you have to pay Federal excise taxes on alcohol, tobacco, or firearm sales.

To get a federal tax ID number, you'll need to complete the IRS form number SS-4 included in this section and send it to the IRS office that is listed in the instructions for the form. Your number will arrive by mail.

Since the bank will need a tax ID number to open your corporate checking account, you'll probably need your tax ID number faster than the IRS can provide it by mail. To get your ID number in a hurry, complete the form SS-4, and then call the telephone number for your area listed in the instructions to the form.

When they answer the phone, tell the person that you'd like to get an Employer ID number by phone. When you reach the person that assigns the ID numbers, they will basically ask you most of the questions on the form, record the information, and give you an ID number. Afterward, you will receive written verification by mail. The IRS form SS-4 and its instructions are at the end of this chapter. Oh by the way, the date of your incorporation will probably be the only date you'll know for sure. *The other dates will be your best estimates.*

State and Local Taxes

State taxes, of course vary from state to state, and are beyond the scope of this book. But, in order to help you, here is a list of many of the state and local taxes you'll encounter. Usually, when you start your corporation the State will notify many of these taxing authorities for you. If you have any questions about state and local taxes, call the city, the county, and the state department of revenue to find out more about them. Their telephone numbers can be found in your telephone directory under the state and local governmental headings. Your local chamber of commerce is usually an ideal one stop source for this information.

- Local business tax/permits

- Special taxes on beer, gas, mining, etc.

- Local general property tax

- Hotel/Motel/Entertainment taxes

- State sales & unemployment tax

- Corporation income/excise tax

Federal Taxes

Other than having to file a corporate income tax return, your most important contact with the Federal government will be withholding taxes. Withholding taxes are what we all have taken out of our hard earned pay every week. Our employer then forwards this money to the government on our behalf. There are three amounts that you will be responsible for paying:

1. Income taxes on employee pay,

2. Social Security (FICA) taxes on employee pay, and

3. FICA matching.

Income taxes and FICA is withheld from employee pay as a percentage of the employee's pay. Basically, when you withhold amounts from your employees pay, you will hold on to the money until the 15th of the next month, at which time you'll deposit the money at your local bank, using a special deposit ticket that the IRS will send you. Plus, at the end of each quarter, you'll file a special with-holding tax return with the IRS.

This procedure is simplified by using publications, and attending workshops that the IRS produces at no charge to you. To obtain publications, or find out when workshops will be held, call the IRS toll free at 1-800-829-1040. At a mini-mum, you should obtain these two free publications:

1. Publication number 937 entitled "Business Reporting", which explains what is required of you as an employer, and

2. A "Circular E", which explains how, and how much to withhold.

The third type of tax you will become familiar with is what's known as FICA match-ing. Whenever you withhold FICA (Social Security) taxes from your employee's pay, you will have to pay that same amount to the government for your "FICA matching". Although painful, it's really simple. If you withhold $25 in Social Secu-rity taxes from an employee's pay one pay period, you'll have to match that $25, and send the government $50, plus the amount of income taxes you withheld for that employee. All these amounts will be deposited on the 15th of the next month.

Accounting and Bookkeeping

One of the areas that small business people have trouble with the most is ac-counting. Accounting can be made as simple or as hard as you want it to be. No matter what you do for an accounting system, do something. Many people are so afraid of accounting and bookkeeping, that they simply neglect it, and that's when trouble begins.

The most important thing about accounting systems is to simply keep good records of how much money you take in, and how much you spend. If you at least do this, you can pay someone to sort through the records at the end of the year. Your records can be as simple as your checkbook register, or as sophisticated as a computerized bookkeeping system. Next, you'll find a list of the items that you will need to keep up with separately.

- Sales

- How much you spent on goods that you resold (cost of goods sold)

- How much you spent on supplies to manufacture your products

- How much you paid employees to manufacture your products

- Compensation of corporate officers, and salaries and wages of employees

- Repairs of any type

- Amounts that were owed to you, included in income, and were not paid

- Rent

- Taxes - State and Local

- Interest

- Depreciation (amounts expensed periodically for cars, equipment, etc.)

- Depletion (for mining, and oil companies)

- Advertising

- Pension and profit sharing plans

- Employee benefit programs (reimbursement plans, paid vacations, etc.)

- Other deductions

"Other deductions" will include anything not otherwise listed. For these, you need to create your own categories like insurance, supplies, and so on. You need to list these expenses separately on your corporate tax return using your own categories. Also, a bit of advice, the IRS doesn't like the term "Misc. Expenses". They want to know exactly what you spent your money on, so don't use the category "Misc." if you can help it.

These categories are taken from a corporate tax return. If all you do is separate, and keep up with the amount of money you spend on the expenses listed above, all you'll need to do at tax time is write the totals on your corporate income tax return. One of the best books on how to set up and run an accounting system is available free from the IRS. Its called "Taxpayers Starting a Business", publication number 583.

CERTIFIED RESOLUTION OF THE BOARD OF DIRECTORS

(For establishing a corporate checking account)

I, _____ do hereby certify that I am the duly elected and qualified Secretary and record keeper of

a corporation organized under the laws of the State of _____, and that the following is a true ant correct copy of certain resolutions duly adopted at a meeting of the Board of Directors thereof, convened and held in accordance with law, the Charter, the Articles of Incorporation, and bylaws of the corporation. The meeting took place on the _____ day of _____ 19___. The resolutions are now in force and are included in the records of the corporation.

It is resolved that _____, (hereinafter referred to as the "bank") will be a financial institution of the corporation, and that an account will be opened in the name of, for and on the behalf of the corporation. The name that the accounts will be opened in will be the same as the corporation name shown above.

It is further resolved that delivery to the bank of funds, checks, drafts, or other property, with or without endorsement, will be deposited to the credit of the corporation, and such credits may be withdrawn by check, draft, or other instrument, executed for the corporation by any _____ of the following individuals.

_____

_____

_____

_____

_____
Secretary

_____
Date

Form **SS-4**
(Rev. December 1993)
Department of the Treasury
Internal Revenue Service

Application for Employer Identification Number

(For use by employers, corporations, partnerships, trusts, estates, churches, government agencies, certain individuals, and others. See instructions.)

EIN

OMB No. 1545-0003
Expires 12-31-96

Please type or print clearly.

1 Name of applicant (Legal name) (See instructions.)

2 Trade name of business, if different from name in line 1

3 Executor, trustee, "care of" name

4a Mailing address (street address) (room, apt., or suite no.)

5a Business address, if different from address in lines 4a and 4b

4b City, state, and ZIP code

5b City, state, and ZIP code

6 County and state where principal business is located

7 Name of principal officer, general partner, grantor, owner, or trustor—SSN required (See instructions.) ▶

8a Type of entity (Check only one box.) (See instructions.)
- ☐ Sole Proprietor (SSN) _____
- ☐ REMIC
- ☐ Personal service corp.
- ☐ State/local government
- ☐ National guard
- ☐ Other nonprofit organization (specify) _____
- ☐ Other (specify) ▶ _____
- ☐ Estate (SSN of decedent) _____
- ☐ Plan administrator-SSN _____
- ☐ Other corporation (specify) _____
- ☐ Federal government/military
- ☐ Church or church controlled organization
- (enter GEN if applicable) _____
- ☐ Trust
- ☐ Partnership
- ☐ Farmers' cooperative

8b If a corporation, name the state or foreign country (if applicable) where incorporated ▶

State

Foreign country

9 Reason for applying (Check only one box.)
- ☐ Started new business (specify) ▶ _____
- ☐ Hired employees
- ☐ Created a pension plan (specify type) ▶ _____
- ☐ Banking purpose (specify) ▶
- ☐ Changed type of organization (specify) ▶ _____
- ☐ Purchased going business
- ☐ Created a trust (specify) ▶ _____
- ☐ Other (specify) ▶

10 Date business started or acquired (Mo., day, year) (See instructions.)

11 Enter closing month of accounting year. (See instructions.)

12 First date wages or annuities were paid or will be paid (Mo., day, year). **Note:** *If applicant is a withholding agent, enter date income will first be paid to nonresident alien. (Mo., day, year)* . . . . ▶

13 Enter highest number of employees expected in the next 12 months. **Note:** *If the applicant does not expect to have any employees during the period, enter "0."* . . . . ▶

Nonagricultural	Agricultural	Household

14 Principal activity (See instructions.) ▶

15 Is the principal business activity manufacturing? . . . . ☐ Yes ☐ No
If "Yes," principal product and raw material used ▶

16 To whom are most of the products or services sold? Please check the appropriate box. ☐ Business (wholesale)
☐ Public (retail) ☐ Other (specify) ▶ ☐ N/A

17a Has the applicant ever applied for an identification number for this or any other business? . . . . ☐ Yes ☐ No
Note: *If "Yes," please complete lines 17b and 17c.*

17b If you checked the "Yes" box in line 17a, give applicant's legal name and trade name, if different than name shown on prior application.

Legal name ▶

Trade name ▶

17c Enter approximate date, city, and state where the application was filed and the previous employer identification number if known.

Approximate date when filed (Mo., day, year)	City and state where filed	Previous EIN

Under penalties of perjury, I declare that I have examined this application, and to the best of my knowledge and belief, it is true, correct, and complete.

Business telephone number (include area code)

Name and title (Please type or print clearly.) ▶

Signature ▶

Date ▶

Note: *Do not write below this line.* For official use only.

Please leave blank ▶	Geo.	Ind.	Class	Size	Reason for applying

For Paperwork Reduction Act Notice, see attached instructions.

Cat. No. 16055N

Form **SS-4** (Rev. 12-93)

General Instructions

(Section references are to the Internal Revenue Code unless otherwise noted.)

Purpose

Use Form SS-4 to apply for an employer identification number (EIN). An EIN is a nine-digit number (for example, 12-3456789) assigned to sole proprietors, corporations, partnerships, estates, trusts, and other entities for filing and reporting purposes. The information you provide on this form will establish your filing and reporting requirements.

Who Must File

You must file this form if you have not obtained an EIN before and

● You pay wages to one or more employees.

● You are required to have an EIN to use on any return, statement, or other document, even if you are not an employer.

● You are a withholding agent required to withhold taxes on income, other than wages, paid to a nonresident alien (individual, corporation, partnership, etc.). A withholding agent may be an agent, broker, fiduciary, manager, tenant, or spouse, and is required to file **Form 1042**, Annual Withholding Tax Return for U.S. Source Income of Foreign Persons.

● You file **Schedule C**, Profit or Loss From Business, or **Schedule F**, Profit or Loss From Farming, of **Form 1040**, U.S. Individual Income Tax Return, and have a Keogh plan or are required to file excise, employment, or alcohol, tobacco, or firearms returns.

The following must use EINs even if they do not have any employees:

● Trusts, except the following:

1. Certain grantor-owned revocable trusts (see the Instructions for Form 1040).

2. Individual Retirement Arrangement (IRA) trusts, unless the trust has to file **Form 990-T**, Exempt Organization Business Income Tax Return (See the Instructions for Form 990-T.)

● Estates

● Partnerships

● REMICS (real estate mortgage investment conduits) (See the instructions for **Form 1066**, U.S. Real Estate Mortgage Investment Conduit Income Tax Return.)

● Corporations

● Nonprofit organizations (churches, clubs, etc.)

● Farmers' cooperatives

● Plan administrators (A plan administrator is the person or group of persons specified as the administrator by the instrument under which the plan is operated.)

Note: *Household employers are not required to file Form SS-4 to get an EIN. An EIN may be assigned to you without filing Form SS-4 if your only employees are household employees (domestic workers) in your private home. To have an EIN assigned to you, write "NONE" in the space for the EIN on* **Form 942,** *Employer's Quarterly Tax Return for Household Employees, when you file it.*

When To Apply for A New EIN

New Business.—If you become the new owner of an existing business, **DO NOT** use the EIN of the former owner. If you already have an EIN, use that number. If you do not have one, apply for one on this form. If you become the "owner" of a corporation by acquiring its stock, use the corporation's EIN.

Changes in Organization or Ownership.—If you already have an EIN, you may need to get a new one if either the organization or ownership of your business changes. If you incorporate a sole proprietorship or form a partnership, you must get a new EIN. However, **DO NOT** apply for a new EIN if you change only the name of your business.

File Only One Form SS-4.—File only one Form SS-4, regardless of the number of businesses operated or trade names under which a business operates. However, each corporation in an affiliated group must file a separate application.

EIN Applied For, But Not Received.—If you do not have an EIN by the time a return is due, write "Applied for" and the date you applied in the space shown for the number. **DO NOT** show your social security number as an EIN on returns.

If you do not have an EIN by the time a tax deposit is due, send your payment to the Internal Revenue service center for your filing area. (See **Where To Apply** below.) Make your check or money order payable to Internal Revenue Service and show your name (as shown on Form SS-4), address, kind of tax, period covered, and date you applied for an EIN.

For more information about EINs, see **Pub. 583**, Taxpayers Starting a Business and **Pub. 1635**, EINs Made Easy.

How To Apply

You can apply for an EIN either by mail or by telephone. You can get an EIN immediately by calling the Tele-TIN phone number for the service center for your state, or you can send the completed Form SS-4 directly to the service center to receive your EIN in the mail.

Application by Tele-TIN.—Under the Tele-TIN program, you can receive your EIN over the telephone and use it immediately to file a return or make a payment. To receive an EIN by phone, complete Form SS-4, then call the Tele-TIN phone number listed for your state under **Where To Apply.** The person making the call must be authorized to sign the form (see **Signature block** on page 3).

An IRS representative will use the information from the Form SS-4 to establish your account and assign you an EIN. Write the number you are given on the upper right-hand corner of the form, sign and date it.

You should mail or FAX the signed SS-4 ***within 24 hours*** *to the Tele-TIN Unit at the service center address for your state.* The IRS representative will give you the FAX number. The FAX numbers are also listed in Pub. 1635.

Taxpayer representatives can receive their client's EIN by phone if they first send a facsimile (FAX) of a completed **Form 2848,** Power of Attorney and Declaration of Representative, or **Form 8821,** Tax Information Authorization, to the Tele-TIN unit. The Form 2848 or Form 8821 will be used solely to release the EIN to the representative authorized on the form.

Application by Mail.—Complete Form SS-4 at least 4 to 5 weeks before you will need an EIN. Sign and date the application and mail it to the service center address for your state. You will receive your EIN in the mail in approximately 4 weeks.

Where To Apply

The Tele-TIN phone numbers listed below will involve a long-distance charge to callers outside of the local calling area, and should be used only to apply for an EIN. THE NUMBERS MAY CHANGE WITHOUT NOTICE. Use 1-800-829-1040 to verify a number or to ask about an application by mail or other Federal tax matters.

If your principal business, office or agency, or legal residence in the case of an individual, is located in:	Call the Tele-TIN phone number shown or file with the Internal Revenue Service center at:
Florida, Georgia, South Carolina	Attn: Entity Control Atlanta, GA 39901 (404) 455-2360
New Jersey, New York City and counties of Nassau, Rockland, Suffolk, and Westchester	Attn: Entity Control Holtsville, NY 00501 (516) 447-4955
New York (all other counties), Connecticut, Maine, Massachusetts, New Hampshire, Rhode Island, Vermont	Attn: Entity Control Andover, MA 05501 (508) 474-9717
Illinois, Iowa, Minnesota, Missouri, Wisconsin	Attn: Entity Control Stop 57A 2306 E. Bannister Rd. Kansas City, MO 64131 (816) 926-5999
Delaware, District of Columbia, Maryland, Pennsylvania, Virginia	Attn: Entity Control Philadelphia, PA 19255 (215) 574-2400

Indiana, Kentucky, Michigan, Ohio, West Virginia	Attn: Entity Control Cincinnati, OH 45999 (606) 292-5467
Kansas, New Mexico, Oklahoma, Texas	Attn: Entity Control Austin, TX 73301 (512) 462-7843
Alaska, Arizona, California (counties of Alpine, Amador, Butte, Calaveras, Colusa, Contra Costa, Del Norte, El Dorado, Glenn, Humboldt, Lake, Lassen, Marin, Mendocino, Modoc, Napa, Nevada, Placer, Plumas, Sacramento, San Joaquin, Shasta, Sierra, Siskiyou, Solano, Sonoma, Sutter, Tehama, Trinity, Yolo, and Yuba), Colorado, Idaho, Montana, Nebraska, Nevada, North Dakota, Oregon, South Dakota, Utah, Washington, Wyoming	Attn: Entity Control Mail Stop 6271-T P.O. Box 9950 Ogden, UT 84409 (801) 620-7645
California (all other counties), Hawaii	Attn: Entity Control Fresno, CA 93888 (209) 452-4010
Alabama, Arkansas, Louisiana, Mississippi, North Carolina, Tennessee	Attn: Entity Control Memphis, TN 37501 (901) 365-5970

If you have no legal residence, principal place of business, or principal office or agency in any state, file your form with the Internal Revenue Service Center, Philadelphia, PA 19255 or call (215) 574-2400.

Specific Instructions

The instructions that follow are for those items that are not self-explanatory. Enter N/A (nonapplicable) on the lines that do not apply.

Line 1.—Enter the legal name of the entity applying for the EIN exactly as it appears on the social security card, charter, or other applicable legal document.

Individuals.—Enter the first name, middle initial, and last name.

Trusts.—Enter the name of the trust.

Estate of a decedent.—Enter the name of the estate.

Partnerships.—Enter the legal name of the partnership as it appears in the partnership agreement.

Corporations.—Enter the corporate name as set forth in the corporation charter or other legal document creating it.

Plan administrators.—Enter the name of the plan administrator. A plan administrator who already has an EIN should use that number.

Line 2.—Enter the trade name of the business if different from the legal name. The trade name is the "doing business as" name.

Note: *Use the full legal name on line 1 on all tax returns filed for the entity. However, if you enter a trade name on line 2 and choose to use the trade name instead of the legal name, enter the trade name on all returns you file. To prevent processing delays and errors, always use either the legal name only or the trade name only on all tax returns.*

Line 3.—Trusts enter the name of the trustee. Estates enter the name of the executor, administrator, or other fiduciary. If the entity applying has a designated person to receive tax information, enter that person's name as the "care of" person. Print or type the first name, middle initial, and last name.

Line 7.—Enter the first name, middle initial, last name, and social security number (SSN) of a principal officer if the business is a corporation; of a general partner if a partnership; and of a grantor owner, or trustor if a trust.

Line 8a.—Check the box that best describes the type of entity applying for the EIN. If not specifically mentioned, check the "other" box and enter the type of entity. Do not enter N/A.

Sole proprietor.—Check this box if you file Schedule C or F (Form 1040) and have a Keogh plan, or are required to file excise, employment, or alcohol, tobacco, or firearms returns. Enter your SSN (social security number) in the space provided.

Plan administrator.—If the plan administrator is an individual, enter the plan administrator's SSN in the space provided.

Withholding agent.—If you are a withholding agent required to file Form 1042, check the "other" box and enter "withholding agent."

REMICs.—Check this box if the entity has elected to be treated as a real estate mortgage investment conduit (REMIC). See the Instructions for Form 1066 for more information.

Personal service corporations.—Check this box if the entity is a personal service corporation. An entity is a personal service corporation for a tax year only if:

● The principal activity of the entity during the testing period (prior tax year) for the tax year is the performance of personal services substantially by employee-owners.

● The employee-owners own 10 percent of the fair market value of the outstanding stock in the entity on the last day of the testing period.

Personal services include performance of services in such fields as health, law, accounting, consulting, etc. For more information about personal service corporations, see the instructions to **Form 1120,** U.S. Corporation Income Tax Return, and **Pub. 542,** Tax Information on Corporations.

Other corporations.—This box is for any corporation other than a personal service corporation. If you check this box, enter the type of corporation (such as insurance company) in the space provided.

Other nonprofit organizations.—Check this box if the nonprofit organization is

other than a church or church-controlled organization and specify the type of nonprofit organization (for example, an educational organization.)

If the organization also seeks tax-exempt status, you must file either **Package 1023** or **Package 1024,** Application for Recognition of Exemption. Get **Pub. 557,** Tax-Exempt Status for Your Organization, for more information.

Group exemption number (GEN).—If the organization is covered by a group exemption letter, enter the four-digit GEN. (Do not confuse the GEN with the nine-digit EIN.) If you do not know the GEN, contact the parent organization. Get Pub. 557 for more information about group exemption numbers.

Line 9.—Check only **one** box. Do not enter N/A.

Started new business.—Check this box if you are starting a new business that requires an EIN. If you check this box, enter the type of business being started. **DO NOT** apply if you already have an EIN and are only adding another place of business.

Changed type of organization.—Check this box if the business is changing its type of organization, for example, if the business was a sole proprietorship and has been incorporated or has become a partnership. If you check this box, specify in the space provided the type of change made, for example, "from sole proprietorship to partnership."

Purchased going business.—Check this box if you purchased an existing business. DO NOT use the former owner's EIN. Use your own EIN if you already have one.

Hired employees.—Check this box if the existing business is requesting an EIN because it has hired or is hiring employees and is therefore required to file employment tax returns. **DO NOT** apply if you already have an EIN and are only hiring employees. If you are hiring household employees, see **Note** under **Who Must File** on page 2.

Created a trust.—Check this box if you created a trust, and enter the type of trust created.

Note: *DO NOT file this form if you are the individual-grantor/owner of a revocable trust. You must use your SSN for the trust. See the instructions for Form 1040.*

Created a pension plan.—Check this box if you have created a pension plan and need this number for reporting purposes. Also, enter the type of plan created.

Banking purpose.—Check this box if you are requesting an EIN for banking purposes only and enter the banking purpose (for example, a bowling league for depositing dues, an investment club for dividend and interest reporting, etc.).

Other (specify).—Check this box if you are requesting an EIN for any reason other than those for which there are checkboxes, and enter the reason.

Line 10.—If you are starting a new business, enter the starting date of the business. If the business you acquired is already operating, enter the date you acquired the business. Trusts should enter the date the trust was legally created. Estates should enter the date of death of the decedent whose name appears on line 1 or the date when the estate was legally funded.

Line 11.—Enter the last month of your accounting year or tax year. An accounting or tax year is usually 12 consecutive months, either a calendar year or a fiscal year (including a period of 52 or 53 weeks). A calendar year is 12 consecutive months ending on December 31. A fiscal year is either 12 consecutive months ending on the last day of any month other than December or a 52-53 week year. For more information on accounting periods, see **Pub. 538,** Accounting Periods and Methods.

Individuals.—Your tax year generally will be a calendar year.

Partnerships.—Partnerships generally must adopt the tax year of either (1) the majority partners; (2) the principal partners; (3) the tax year that results in the least aggregate (total) deferral of income; or (4) some other tax year. (See the Instructions for **Form 1065,** U.S. Partnership Return of Income, for more information.)

REMICs.—Remics must have a calendar year as their tax year.

Personal service corporations.—A personal service corporation generally must adopt a calendar year unless:

● It can establish a business purpose for having a different tax year, or

● It elects under section 444 to have a tax year other than a calendar year.

Trusts.—Generally, a trust must adopt a calendar year except for the following:

● Tax-exempt trusts,

● Charitable trusts, and

● Grantor-owned trusts.

Line 12.—If the business has or will have employees, enter the date on which the business began or will begin to pay wages. If the business does not plan to have employees, enter N/A.

Withholding agent.—Enter the date you began or will begin to pay income to a nonresident alien. This also applies to individuals who are required to file Form 1042 to report alimony paid to a nonresident alien.

Line 14.—Generally, enter the exact type of business being operated (for example, advertising agency, farm, food or beverage establishment, labor union, real estate agency, steam laundry, rental of coin-operated vending machine, investment club, etc.). Also state if the business will involve the sale or distribution of alcoholic beverages.

Governmental.—Enter the type of organization (state, county, school district, or municipality, etc.).

Nonprofit organization (other than governmental).—Enter whether organized for religious, educational, or humane purposes, and the principal activity (for example, religious organization—hospital, charitable).

Mining and quarrying.—Specify the process and the principal product (for example, mining bituminous coal, contract drilling for oil, quarrying dimension stone, etc.).

Contract construction.—Specify whether general contracting or special trade contracting. Also, show the type of work normally performed (for example, general contractor for residential buildings, electrical subcontractor, etc.).

Food or beverage establishments.—Specify the type of establishment and state whether you employ workers who receive tips (for example, lounge—yes).

Trade.—Specify the type of sales and the principal line of goods sold (for example, wholesale dairy products, manufacturer's representative for mining machinery, retail hardware, etc.).

Manufacturing.—Specify the type of establishment operated (for example, sawmill, vegetable cannery, etc.).

Signature block.—The application must be signed by: (1) the individual, if the applicant is an individual, (2) the president, vice president, or other principal officer, if the applicant is a corporation, (3) a responsible and duly authorized member or officer having knowledge of its affairs, if the applicant is a partnership or other unincorporated organization, or (4) the fiduciary, if the applicant is a trust or estate.

Some Useful Publications

You may get the following publications for additional information on the subjects covered on this form. To get these and other free forms and publications, call 1-800-TAX-FORM (1-800-829-3676).

Pub. 1635, EINs Made Easy

Pub. 538, Accounting Periods and Methods

Pub. 541, Tax Information on Partnerships

Pub. 542, Tax Information on Corporations

Pub. 557, Tax-Exempt Status for Your Organization

Pub. 583, Taxpayers Starting A Business

Pub. 937, Employment Taxes and Information Returns

Package 1023, Application for Recognition of Exemption

Package 1024, Application for Recognition of Exemption Under Section 501(a) or for Determination Under Section 120

Paperwork Reduction Act Notice

We ask for the information on this form to carry out the Internal Revenue laws of the United States. You are required to give us the information. We need it to ensure that you are complying with these laws and to allow us to figure and collect the right amount of tax.

The time needed to complete and file this form will vary depending on individual circumstances. The estimated average time is:

Recordkeeping . . . . . . 7 min.

Learning about the law or the form . . . . . . 18 min.

Preparing the form . . . . 44 min.

Copying, assembling, and sending the form to the IRS . 20 min.

If you have comments concerning the accuracy of these time estimates or suggestions for making this form more simple, we would be happy to hear from you. You can write to both the **Internal Revenue Service,** Attention: Reports Clearance Officer, PC:FP, Washington, DC 20224; and the **Office of Management and Budget,** Paperwork Reduction Project (1545-0003), Washington, DC 20503. **DO NOT** send this form to either of these offices. Instead, see **Where To Apply** on page 2.

10

THE INCORPORATING PROCESS

The Secretary of State has general supervision of corporations in Illinois. The Corporation Division is the specific office in the Secretary of State's office that actually sets up and regulates the corporations. You will work with the Secretary of State now, and in the future when you need to make changes, or do something that requires the retrieving of recorded documents. Everyone we've spoken to at the Secretary of State's office is very helpful and friendly. They can answer most any question you may have about forming a corporation.

The corporation division's office is in Springfield. Their office hours are from 8-4:30 Monday-Friday. You may either mail, or hand deliver your documents to their office. If you hand deliver your documents and wait for them to be processed there is an additional charge of $50 for expedited handling. Otherwise, it will take about a week for your documents to be processed. No paperwork is accepted after 4:00 p.m. Their telephone number and address are as follows:

Secretary of State
Corporation Division
Howlett Building
Room 328
Springfield, IL 62756   Telephone 217-782-9522 or 782-9523 or 782-6961

There is a satellite office in Chicago. The phone number is (312) 793-3380

QUESTIONS ABOUT ILLINOIS

What's the Least Number of People Needed to Incorporate?
ONE. All officer and director positions may be held by one person.

How Many Directors does the Corporation Need?
At least one. Directors manage the business affairs for the corporation, and enjoy some immunity from certain actions. All important business decisions should be made, and recorded as made, by the directors. Directors need not be residents of the State nor shareholders.

How Many Officers does the Corporation Need?
ONE. You should have all four officer positions filled, but all of these positions may be held by the same person.

Must Incorporators Meet Certain Requirements?
State law has no particular requirements for incorporators. However, the incorporator should be at least 18 years of age.

Is There a Certain Amount of Capital Required?
No. Some states require that you put a certain amount of money or property into the corporation before you can incorporate, but Illinois does not.

THE INCORPORATION PROCESS

The incorporation process is very simple, and consists of six basic steps. Steps two and three are the only steps that involve the Secretary of State, the other steps are completed with the other shareholders, directors, and officers. Please read all of the steps and understand them fully before completing any step. A mistake could result in having to redo and refile paperwork, costing time and money. Before proceeding, read the introduction to this book, then call the Secretary of State and ask them to send you a current fee schedule.

STEP 1   Choose a corporate name.
STEP 2   Check the availability of the name.
STEP 3   File your paperwork.
STEP 4   Organizational matters.
STEP 5   Issue the stock of the corporation.
STEP 6   Prepare a corporate record book.

Step 1.

Choose a Corporate Name

The first step in organizing your corporation is selecting a name. The corporate name must meet specific requirements outlined by State law. Specifically, your corporate name must meet the following criteria:

1. It should not be misleading to the public.
2. It must be distinguishable from other corporate names.
3. It should contain either incorporated, corporation or an abbreviation thereof.

To satisfy the *first requirement*, your corporate name should not include language either stating or implying that the corporation is something it's not. A corporate name should not imply that the corporation is empowered to transact any business for which authorization is required by Illinois law unless the authorization is officially granted to the business and the authorization is certified in writing. For example, if you're not a CPA, don't use CPA as part of your corporate name.

A corporate name may not imply that the corporation is affiliated with, or sponsored by, any fraternal, veteran's, service, religious, charitable, or professional organization unless the authorization is officially granted to the business and the authorization is certified in writing. For example, if you're not part of the YMCA, don't imply it.

Finally, a corporate name may not imply that the corporation is associated with, or sponsored by a state government, the federal government or a branch thereof, unless the authorization is officially granted to the business and the authorization is certified in writing. For example, stay away from names that make your corporation sound like it's a part of the State or Federal government. Although using the word federal in your name is usually okay, be careful not to imply any governmental authority or affiliation to your name.

The main point to remember is that your name should not be confusing or misleading to the public. Accordingly, your corporate name should reflect the nature of the business you plan to conduct. For example, the name Consumer Publishing, Inc. tells you that we produce consumer related publications.

The *second requirement* your corporate name must meet is this. It must be distinguishable from other corporate names on record with the Secretary of State. This requirement is almost self-explanatory. Simply, your name may not be the same as another corporate name already being used in Illinois. Letting more than one corporation use the same name would be confusing to the public and possibly damaging to the company that held initial claim to the name. In addition, allowing more than one company to use the same name would lead to difficulties when filing lawsuits against a corporation.

The next step will discuss how to see if the name you like is already being used. For now, you need to decide exactly what your corporate name will be, and come up with a couple of alternatives in case your first choice is unavailable. The telephone book is an excellent place to shop for a name, remembering of course that your name must also be distinguishable from the names found there.

When choosing your name, care must be taken if the name you prefer is a common one. Because if it is, someone is probably already using it. For example, if you wanted to name your corporation Brown, Inc., you may not be able to. The name Brown is so common, it was probably taken long ago. However, if your name is Brown and you wanted to use it in your business, there is still a way to do it. All you need to do is change the name slightly, just enough to "distinguish" it from others. For example, instead of using Brown, Inc., you could add your first name or initial, and name your corporation William Brown, Inc., or D. Brown, Inc. Alternatively, you could add a descriptive word or two, and name the corporation like the following examples.

The *third requirement* your corporate name must meet is an easy one to satisfy. All you have to do is include as a part of your corporate name, one of the following words. Let's refer to them as "Inc." words.

Incorporated, or its abbreviation, *Inc.*
Corporation, or its abbreviation, *Corp.*

These Inc. words distinguish a business as a corporation. Below are some of the possible uses of these terms. You can tell by their names that the businesses in this list are incorporated.

Brown *Incorporated*	Brown, *Inc.*
The Brown *Corporation*	The Brown *Corp.*
Brown & Company, *Inc.*	The Brown *Corporation, Inc.*

Please note that simply changing the "Inc." word does not make a corporate name distinguishable. That is, Brown Incorporated, Brown, Inc., Brown Corporation, and Brown Corp. are not distinguishable since the only difference is the "Inc." word.

Step 2.

Check the Availability of "Your" Name

Now that you've chosen the name you wish to use, you'll need to see if another corporation in the state is already using it. To do this, call the office of the Secretary of State at 217-782-9520. Checking the availability of "your" name should only take a couple of minutes, and this is also a good time to ask any questions that you may have. You will probably be transferred to the main number for any questions not regarding names.

Before you call, be sure of the name you wish to use, and that it contains one of the required "Inc." words. Also, you should have one or two additional names chosen, in case your first choice is being used by another corporation. The Secretary of State has access to all corporate names being used by corporations in the state. The role playing outlined below is designed for a telephone call, but of course face to face conversation will be the same. The conversation will basically go like this:

Sec. State:	Secretary of State's Office, may I help you?
You:	Yes. I'd like to check the availability of a corporate name please. (The person will either check the name, or transfer you to the person who will.)
Sec State:	Okay. What is the name you'd like to check?
You:	Brown Advertising, Inc. (The person will now check their computer for the name.)
Sec State:	That name appears to be available. (That's what you want to hear.)
You:	Thank You.

The Secretary of State will usually only say something to the effect that the "name appears to be available". That's because someone may walk into their office five minutes later and file paperwork using "your" name. There are no guarantees as to the availability of a name until your paperwork is accepted. The name will not be officially yours until either an application to reserve the name, or Articles Of Incorporation is accepted by the State. If you're first choice for a corporate name is already being used, the conversation will usually continue like this:

Sec State: Brown Advertising does *not* appear to be available at this time. Are there any other names you'd like to check? (This is when your second and third choices come in handy.)

You: Yes. What about Brown *& Associates* Advertising, Inc.?

Sec State: (The person will now check for the new name.) That name *does* appear to be available at this time (You've hit pay dirt.)

You: Thank You.

Now that you've learned at least one of your names is available, you have two choices:

1. Reserve the name for your future use, or
2. File your Articles of Incorporation

The first choice should be made if you are not ready to file your incorporation paperwork. To reserve the name, you must file a special application that reserves the name for your exclusive use for a ninety day period. It's called APPLICATION FOR RESERVATION OF CORPORATE NAME, and is included in this section. If you are not ready to incorporate, and are concerned about losing "your" name, your only choice is to file the application to reserve the name. Currently, the fee charged by the Secretary of State to file this application is twenty-five dollars.

Your second choice is to immediately file your incorporation paperwork, a form known as the Articles Of Incorporation, included in this section. Since there is the additional fee charged to reserve the name, most people simply "lock up" their name by filing the Articles Of Incorporation. Any delay in filing one of these documents may cost you "your" name.

Step 3.

File Your Paperwork

The paperwork you must file to incorporate a business in Illinois consists of a one page form, included with this kit, called the Articles Of Incorporation. The Articles are very simple to complete if you know some basic information like your name, the corporation's name, and your address. You should type the form, because typing helps insure its correct recording, and reduces the chance of your Articles being returned because of poor penmanship. The instructions:

Article 1: Insert your corporate name in the space provided. Make sure it meets the specified requirements.

Article 2: Unless you want someone else to be your registered agent, put your name, street address, and county here. The registered office is where all legal correspondence will be sent.

Article 3: In this article, type this statement.

"The transaction of any or all lawful purposes for which corporations may be incorporated under the Illinois Business corporation Act of 1983."

This statement allows the corporation to operate any business it chooses without being restricted to a single activity.

Article 4: The information used in this article is used to calculate part of your filing fee known as the franchise tax. The tax is 15/100 of 1 percent of the total amount of stock initially issued. That means that the franchise tax due when you file will equal the total amount of consideration (money) given for the stock multiplied by .0015. There is a minimum franchise fee of $25 for which you can issue up to 10,000 shares. Accordingly, you should have no more than 10,000 shares unless you want to increase your filing fees.

To complete this article, do the following:

1. Under the heading "Class" put the word "common". This means that you will have common stock as opposed to preferred stock. Preferred stock is more like a bond in that it has a fixed dividend percentage that the shareholder must be paid each quarter and no voting rights.

2. Under the heading "Par value per share" put "n/a." This means that your stock will have no par value which means that you are not stuck with a fixed amount that you must issue stock for. This will give you flexability in accepting payment for stock.

3. The "Number of authorized shares" should be 10,000, the maxumum number that you can have for the $25 minimum franchise fee.

4. The "Number of shares proposed to be issued" is the total number that you will issue to the *initial* shareholders. This does *not* include stock issued after the articles of incorporation have been filed.

5. The "Consideration to be received" is the amount of money plus the value of any property given in exchange for the stock *initially* issued. The amount of consideration given will be the basis on which your franchise tax will be calculated. For a discussion on these subjects see step five.

Paragraph 2:   In "Paragraph 2" of article 4, type this statement:

"The shares of the corporation are of one class, that being no par value common stock, with identical rights and privileges, the transfer of which is restricted according to the Bylaws of the corporation."

Article 5:   Leave this blank.

Article 6:   Leave this blank.

Article 7:   Leave this blank.

Article 8:   Type your name and address on the appropriate lines.

After completing the Articles and double checking them for accuracy, you will need to sign and date them with black ink. All those involved in the corporation do not need to sign the Articles because the Articles will be formally adopted by all shareholders and directors after the Articles return from the Secretary of State's Office. So, only the person completing the Articles (the incorporator) needs to sign.

Now you are ready to file your Articles. You will send the Secretary of State the original Articles, an exact copy, and the filing fees that total one hundred ($100) dollars. The fees consist of seventy-five dollars for filing fees and twenty-five dollars for the minimum franchise tax. The minimum franchise tax is due when less than $10,000 is received for the issuance of stock.

The franchise tax is for the privilege of being a corporation, and is based on the total amount of money received by the corporation for its stock. Although our books are printed in small numbers so that we can keep the information current, you may want to verify the amount of the fees before you file your paperwork. If you verify the fees, the person helping you will need to know the total amount of money, and/or the value of any property, given for the stock initially issued. Finally, send or take these items to the following address:

1. The Cover Letter
2. The original Articles,
3. An exact copy of the completed Articles,
4. A certified check or money order for $100.00, made payable to the Secretary of State. You should include the corporate name and your business phone number on the check.

Secretary of State
Corporation Division
Centennial Building
Room 328
Springfield, IL 62756

If you reserved your name prior to filing the Articles, you should bring this to the Secretary of State's attention when you file the Articles. You should do this in order to eliminate any confusion as to who has the right to use the name. To do this, simply write a note, or include a cover letter stating that you reserved the name for the corporation. You should also include any official notification of your name reservation, keeping a copy for yourself.

When the documents are processed, the Secretary of State will time and date stamp your Articles. They will keep the original Articles for their files, and return the copy to you along with official notification of your incorporation. These items will be sent to the address on the Articles. Within 15 days after the Secretary of State mails the copy of your articles to you, the articles must be recorded with the Office of the Recorder of Deeds in the county in which the registered office is located. To do this, simply take everything received from the state to the Recorder of Deeds and tell the clerk that you need to have the Articles of Incorporation recorded. They will charge a small fee for this service. Recording your Articles with the Recorder of Deeds makes your incorporation a matter of public record at the county level.

Step 4.

Organizational Matters

State law requires that after Articles of Incorporation are filed, a few other important details must be taken care of before the organization of your corporation is complete. To mention a few, you must officially adopt the articles and bylaws, elect officers, approve the corporate seal and issue stock. These actions are usually taken at a meeting known as the organizational meeting. At the organizational meeting, all proposed directors, officers, and shareholders meet to discuss these organizational matters, take action on them and record the results as "minutes" of the meeting.

To make this easier than it sounds, a prewritten minutes of directors meeting has been included in this book for your use. The form is called *"Minutes of the Organizational Meeting of the Board of Directors."* If you use this form, all you'll need to do is read it carefully and insert the information pertaining to your corporation in the appropriate blanks.

Of course, most small corporations will only have one or two people acting as all the directors, officers and stockholders. That's fine. I would suggest, however, that you fill at least two of the officer positions—those of president and secretary. A president is needed to run the day-to-day operations of the corporation, like hiring, firing, dealing with the accountant, signing contracts, etc. The secretary is needed to keep up with the internal corporate paperwork—meeting minutes, issuing stock certificates, and drafting corporate resolutions. It's okay for one person to serve as both president and secretary.

If you haven't decided what the officer salaries will be, put a nominal figure of let's say, $100 per year for now. When you decide what the salaries will be, you'll need to hold a directors meeting on the subject. The directors will officially approve of the salary, and this approval will be noted in the minutes of the meeting. In reality, most people simply pay themselves whatever they can. Then, at the end of the year (at tax time), part of the total amount paid is allocated to officer salary and the rest to "regular" salary. The allocation is usually based on the amount of time spent performing officer duties relative to the time spent at other tasks. For example, if you paid yourself $50,000 and spent 10% of your time performing officer duties, then it would be reasonable to pay yourself a $5,000 officer salary and a $45,000 salary for your other efforts. (.10 X $50,000 = $5,000 and $50,000 - $5,000 = $45,000) You may want to speak with your accountant about this. Since the issuance of stock is covered in the next step, don't complete the last section of the minutes entitled *"Stock"* until you have reviewed step five.

Step 5.

Issue the Stock of the Corporation

A business corporation cannot exist without stockholders. Stockholders, or shareholders as they are often called, invest money in a corporation in exchange for a part or "share" of the corporation. In return for their investment, shareholders receive dividends based on the future earnings of the corporation or some other monetary reward. In many cases, shareholders invest in a corporation hoping that its value will increase and enable them to later sell their stock at a profit. Shareholders who buy stock in a corporation for its profit potential are known as investors. Shareholders like yourself who are not investors usually work for the corporation and receive a salary in addition to or instead of dividends.

There are basically two ways to buy stock in a corporation—either directly from the corporation or in the open market. Initially, all stocks are purchased directly from the corporation that issued them. However, many shares are bought by investors who will sell them at some point in the future. This is how shares become available in the open market—investors selling them to other investors. There is such a demand for these shares as investments, huge exchanges like the New York Stock Exchange were created to facilitate the purchase and sell of these secondhand securities.

Unlike the investor who buys for speculation, you are buying stock in your corporation to start a company. Like most small business owners, you'll probably hold on to your stock and someday leave it to your kids. But, like the investor, you will still have to "purchase" the stock from your corporation and give something of value for it. You must bargain with the board of directors to determine a price acceptable to both you and the board. Your situation is a little different because you will play both the role of the prospective shareholder wanting to buy stock and the director wanting to receive something of acceptable value for it. In reality, however, prospective shareholders like yourself will give what they can afford for the stock and of course "the board" will accept your offer. In this case the issuance of stock boils down to three things:

- Who will the shareholders be?
- How many shares or what percent of the corporation will each person own?
- How much will the shareholders pay for each share of stock?

Once you know the answers to these questions, issuing the stock is simply a matter of completing the last section of the form entitled "Minutes of the Organizational Meeting of the Board of Directors" and issuing stock certificates to each new shareholder. Be sure to read the remainder of this section before issuing the stock. Also, remember the price per share of all initially issued shares must be the same.

Stock Registration

If you are starting a business and wish to attract investors by incorporating, are trying to make money from the sale of the stock, or will be paying commissions to a broker for the sale of the stock, you will need to register your stock with the Securities Division of The Secretary of State's office. The telephone number is (217) 782-2256.

If you offer your stock to someone living outside Illinois, your stock issue will fall under Federal securities laws as an interstate offering. If you plan to make such an out of State offer, you may want to seek professional advice. If you don't want to "seek professional advice" make sure that the person to whom you are offering stock is standing on Illinois soil at the time of the offer. This makes the offering an intrastate offering, regulated by State securities law.

The registration of securities, stocks, bonds, partnership interests, etc., is a process designed to protect investors from fraudulent securities offerings. It involves the gathering of information related to the offering, and the drafting of a document called a prospectus. A prospectus is an informational booklet designed to give investors enough information about the company and the offering to make an informed buying decision. Under the securities laws of Illinois, some stock offerings are exempt from registration while others are not. If you are simply incorporating your existing business or issuing stock to family members or other organizers and officers of the corporation that live in Illinois, state law provides for you an exemption from registration. Generally, the issuance of stock is exempt from registration if:

1. The stock is only issued to officers and organizers of the corporation.
2. The stock is issued by the corporation and not a securities dealer.
3. The issue is not advertised or offered to the general public. (Outsiders)
4. There are fewer than 35 shareholders when all the stock is issued.
   (Husband and wife count as one shareholder.)

The main point to remember is this. Registration is designed to protect consumers from fraudulent stock offerings. So, do NOT offer stock to someone unless they are intimately familiar with the financial condition of the corporation.

Authorized VS. Issued Shares

If you conclude your stock is exempt from registration, you may proceed with its issue. But before you issue stock, let's discuss the difference between authorized shares of stock and issued shares of stock. Authorized shares is the number of shares set by the Articles of Incorporation that the board of directors is "authorized" to issue. The board of directors is the body that controls the issuance of stock. In large corporations, this authorized limit on the total number of shares prevents the board from issuing too many shares. Too many new shares lowers the value of your stock.

The board may issue all the shares now, or issue some now, and some later. Your Articles of Incorporation, state the number of shares that the corporation is authorized to issue and make this number a matter of public record for all to see. The number of authorized shares equals the total number of shares that may be issued now, or at some point in the future. Issued shares is the number of shares "issued", or distributed to shareholders. Only issued shares count for ownership purposes. Shares that are not issued are called authorized but unissued shares. They are technically worthless until they are issued to a shareholder. Usually when a corporation issues shares of stock to its initial shareholders, a few shares are left unissued so that they may be issued later to new investors, family members etc.

It is a good idea not to issue (distribute) all of the authorized shares now, because you may need a few shares to issue later. You may want to issue some stock to a son or daughter entering the business, or to a new business partner. The main point to remember is that only *issued* shares count for ownership percentages. Take the following example for a corporation that has 1000 *authorized* (another word for available) shares of stock, and two owners. An example:

Owner A is issued 100 shares 100/200=50% ownership
(Number owned divided by total issued.)

Owner B is issued 100 shares   100/200=50% ownership
(Number owned divided by total issued.)

The two shareholders in the previous example own 50% of the corporation because the 800 unissued shares are not considered in the calculation. One thousand authorized shares less 200 issued shares leaves 800 available for future use. Since only the 200 issued shares count for ownership, owners with 100 shares each own one half of the corporation. (One hundred is half of two hundred.)

Consideration

Stock in a corporation represents various rights and privileges to the shareholder. So, in exchange for the stock of a corporation something of value must be given. The payment given to a corporation for its stock is known as consideration. The type of consideration you give for your stock is governed by state law. You can pay money, give property, or have already provided labor or services to the corporation for which you were not paid.

Since there is no minimum capital requirement in Illinois, any amount of consideration approved by the Board of Directors is acceptable. This amount can be all cash, all property, all services, or various combinations of the three. Since giving consideration other than money can cause tax problems, you should see your CPA before doing so. However, I wouldn't see my CPA if I were simply putting a computer and some office furniture into the corporation. A CPA should be consulted if you are going to put vehicles, buildings, expensive equipment, or other big dollar items into the corporation.

Please note that money given to the corporation doesn't "disappear". In reality, the corporation will spend this much money just opening its doors and you would have put money into the corporation anyway. The corporation will spend this amount reimbursing you for filing fees, taxes, buying office supplies, printing stationery, paying rent and so forth.

If your initial cash contribution isn't enough to get the corporation up and running, you'll have to put more money into the corporation from time to time. If you do, you can account for this contribution in three ways:

1. You can put money into the corporation in return for additional stock. This is usually done when other business associates are involved. (Partners)

2. You can put money into the corporation, issue no more stock and simply call this an owner's contribution. This is usually done when there is only one shareholder. This money is not taxed when taken out of the corporation.

3. You can put money into the corporation, call it a loan, and receive the money back with interest. Discuss this with your CPA first.

If you give property for the stock, you'll need to transfer the title of the property to the corporation, and provide a bill of sale. If there is not enough room to record the payment on the director's minutes, use an additional sheet of paper, and file it with your corporate records. This is a corporate matter that doesn't involve the State. Sometimes, giving property or services for your corporation's stock leads to tax problems, and you should see your CPA accordingly. Fortunately, this is not usually the case.

If you simply give property to your new corporation in exchange for at least 80% of the stock, you usually don't have to worry about taxes. Internal Revenue Code § 351 calls this a tax-free exchange and allows it. However, exchanging property in the following cases will lead to problems. If you want to exchange property for stock in a manner similar to any of these examples, or are transferring property to the corporation to avoid taxes, see your CPA or tax advisor first.

A list of property transfers to avoid:

- An exchange of property to a corporation when you will own less than eighty percent of the stock.

- An exchange where you receive cash, or property, or benefits other than stock for your property.

- An exchange where your liabilities against the property exceed your adjusted basis in that property.

Stock Certificates

Although stock certificates are not money and this is only an analogy, you may compare stock certificates to checks in a checkbook and authorized shares to the amount of money in your checking account. Stock certificates and checks are similar but of course are not the same. Instead of representing money like checks do, stock certificates represent shares of ownership in a corporation. When you write a check, you give someone money. When you issue certificates, you give someone ownership in your corporation. With a checkbook, you can write checks in any dollar amount to as many people as you want until you either run out of money or out of checks. With stock, you can issue certificates for any number of shares to as many people as you want until you either run out of authorized shares or out of certificates.

Please note that you are not limited to using the four certificates included with this book. You can use as many stock certificates as you like. Only four certificates are included in this book because most corporations are one or two person corporations and therefore only need one or two certificates. If you need more, certificates like the ones in the book are available from us for a nominal charge. Also, most corporate kits come with twenty stock certificates custom imprinted with your corporate name.

To issue stock certificates to each shareholder, you must complete the face of the certificate by typing the name of the corporation, the name of the shareholder, the date, and the number of shares in their appropriate spaces. Next, number the certificates sequentially, (01, 02, 03, 04, 05) and have the President and Secretary of the corporation sign the certificates at the bottom on either side of the gold circle. The gold circle is where you will press the corporation's seal. The back of the certificate should also be completed by inserting the corporate name, the shareholder's name, and the issue date in the appropriate places located in the center of the certificate. Do *not* complete the section on the left that begins with "For value received". This section is completed when, and if you ever sell your stock. Completing this section is similar to endorsing a check, and could make the certificate a negotiable instrument.

Type these legends somewhere on the face of the certificate. Total authorized issue is the number of shares that your corporation is authorized to issue. Replace the ? in the third item below with the number of authorized shares your corporation will have.

A ILLINOIS CORPORATION
RESTRICTED, UNREGISTERED STOCK
TOTAL AUTHORIZED ISSUE IS __?__ SHARES WITHOUT PAR VALUE

Step 6

Prepare a Corporate Record Book

Organizing and maintaining the records of the corporation is required by State law and of major importance to the IRS, so do not skip this step. This step is an integral part of incorporating your business properly. Since you are required to keep meticulous records of the activities of your corporation, you will need to set up and maintain a corporate record book. More commonly called a corporate "kit", your corporate record book will contain all the important records of the corporation as well as the corporate seal. For bankers, the IRS and other entities interested in the validity of your corporation, the corporate record book is the only proof that your corporation is properly organized and maintained.

Your corporate kit can be as simple as a three ring indexed binder or a fully customized corporate kit. In preparing a corporate record book, you have two choices, either prepare your own, or purchase one.

If you choose to purchase one and are unable to find corporate supplies in your area, corporate kits and corporate seals are available through Consumer Publishing. Made for us by the country's largest supplier of corporate kits, these kits are the same as those used by lawyers. You can either use your credit card and order by calling 1-800-677-2462, or send a check with the order form at of the book. Corporate kits are shipped within 24 hours. Next day service is also available. Corporate kits are available for C and S corporations as well as non-profit corporations, professional corporations, and close corporations.
Each corporate kit includes:

- A deluxe binder with the corporate name gold embossed on the spine,
- A matching slip case to protect your records from dust,
- A corporate seal,

- 20 Stock certificates imprinted with the corporate name,
- A stock transfer ledger,
- Preprinted minutes and bylaws,
- A special forms section and a review of IRS requirements for S corporations,
- Medical and dental reimbursement plans described in CHAPTER 3,
- Annual meeting forms.

If you prefer to prepare your own corporate kit, you'll need to visit a legal stationary or lawyer supply store and purchase the following:

A three ring binder,
At least 8 tabbed index dividers to divide the book into sections,
Pre-punched three ring binder paper to keep minutes on,
A corporate seal.

A corporate seal should be included with the corporate record book because the seal is how the corporation "signs" contracts, minutes, and other official documents like stock certificates. The seal is maintained by the corporate secretary and is used to show that the corporation approves of documents that the seal is applied to.

After you have all of your supplies together, you should assemble them as follows. First, prepare these headings for the tabbed index dividers; APPLICATIONS & PERMITS; STATE FILINGS; BYLAWS; MINUTES; STOCK CERTIFICATES; S-ELECTION; FORMS; and JOURNAL LEDGER.

Second, three hole punch the documents already filed with the state and/or the IRS, as well as the directors meeting minutes completed in steps 4 & 5 and insert them into the appropriate sections of the corporate record book. Third, copy or remove the bylaws from CHAPTER 7 and insert them into the BYLAWS section. Fourth, copy or remove the prewritten minute forms from CHAPTER 8 and insert them into the MINUTES section. Remember to make copies of the blank originals for your future minute keeping needs. The minutes from all your meetings will be kept in this section. Finally, prepare a separate list of stockholders, directors, and officers of the corporation and include these lists in the JOURNAL LEDGER section. These lists may seem insignificant but are required by law.

APPLICATION FOR RESERVATION OF CORPORATE NAME

Pursuant to Illinois State Law, the undersigned individual submits the following application to reserve a corporate name:

1. The undersigned is the incorporator, and hereby applies for reservation of the following corporate name for the period of time allowed by State Law.

2. The applicant is an individual that meets the age requirements set by State law.

3. The name and street address of the applicant including the zip code are as follows:

4. The corporate name proposed for reservation meets the requirements of State Law.

5. The corporate name to be reserved is:

The undersigned individual hereby declares, under penalty of perjury, that the statements made in the forgoing application are true.

Date:

Name of Applicant:

Signature of Applicant:

Copyright © 1994 Consumer Corporation

COVER LETTER

FROM:

Name of corporation:

Street address of the corporation:

DEAR CORPORATION SERVICES DIVISION:

Please find enclosed:

1. An original Articles of Incorporation and one copy for the above named corporation.
2. A certified check or money order in the amount of $_____ for filing fees.

Please send responses or receipts concerning this filing to the above address.

Thank you very much.

Date:

Name of Incorporator:

Signature of Incorporator:

Form **BCA-2.10**	**ARTICLES OF INCORPORATION**	

(Rev. Jan. 1995)

George H. Ryan
Secretary of State
Department of Business Services
Springfield, IL 62756

This space for use by Secretary of State

SUBMIT IN DUPLICATE!

This space for use by Secretary of State

Date

Franchise Tax $

Filing Fee $

Approved:

Payment must be made by certified check, cashier's check, Illinois attorney's check, Illinois C.P.A's check or money order, payable to "Secretary of State."

1. CORPORATE NAME: _____

_____

(The corporate name must contain the word "corporation", "company," "incorporated," "limited" or an abbreviation thereof.)

2. Initial Registered Agent: _____

First Name	*Middle Initial*	*Last name*

Initial Registered Office: _____

Number	*Street*	*Suite #*

IL

City	*Zip Code*	*County*

3. Purpose or purposes for which the corporation is organized:
(If not sufficient space to cover this point, add one or more sheets of this size.)

4. Paragraph 1: Authorized Shares, Issued Shares and Consideration Received:

Class	Par Value per Share	Number of Shares Authorized	Number of Shares Proposed to be Issued	Consideration to be Received Therefor
	$			$
				TOTAL = $

Paragraph 2: The preferences, qualifications, limitations, restrictions and special or relative rights in respect of the shares of each class are:
(If not sufficient space to cover this point, add one or more sheets of this size.)

(over)

5. *OPTIONAL:*   (a) Number of directors constituting the initial board of directors of the corporation:_____ .

              (b) Names and addresses of the persons who are to serve as directors until the first annual meeting of shareholders or until their successors are elected and qualify:

Name	Residential Address	City, State, ZIP

6. *OPTIONAL:*   (a) It is estimated that the value of all property to be owned by the corporation for the following year wherever located will be: $_____

              (b) It is estimated that the value of the property to be located within the State of Illinois during the following year will be: $_____

              (c) It is estimated that the gross amount of business that will be transacted by the corporation during the following year will be: $_____

              (d) It is estimated that the gross amount of business that will be transacted from places of business in the State of Illinois during the following year will be: $_____

7. *OPTIONAL:*   OTHER PROVISIONS

              Attach a separate sheet of this size for any other provision to be included in the Articles of Incorporation, e.g., authorizing preemptive rights, denying cumulative voting, regulating internal affairs, voting majority requirements, fixing a duration other than perpetual, etc.

8.   **NAME(S) & ADDRESS(ES) OF INCORPORATOR(S)**

The undersigned incorporator(s) hereby declare(s), under penalties of perjury, that the statements made in the foregoing Articles of Incorporation are true.

Dated _____ , 19 _____ .

Signature and Name	**Address**

1. _____
    Signature
	1. _____
	    Street

_____
    (Type or Print Name)
	_____
	    City/Town *State* *Zip Code*

2. _____
    Signature
	2. _____
	    Street

_____
    (Type or Print Name)
	_____
	    City/Town *State* *Zip Code*

3. _____
    Signature
	3. _____
	    Street

_____
    (Type or Print Name)
	_____
	    City/Town *State* *Zip Code*

(Signatures must be in **BLACK INK** on original document. Carbon copy, photocopy or rubber stamp signatures may only be used on conformed copies.)

NOTE: If a corporation acts as incorporator, the name of the corporation and the state of incorporation shall be shown and the execution shall be by its president or vice president and verified by him, and attested by its secretary or assistant secretary.

FEE SCHEDULE

- The initial franchise tax is assessed at the rate of 15/100 of 1 percent ($1.50 per $1,000) on the paid-in capital represented in this state, with a minimum of $25.
- The filing fee is $75.
- The **minimum total due** (franchise tax + filing fee) is **$100.**
  (Applies when the Consideration to be Received as set forth in Item 4 does not exceed $16,667)
- The Department of Business Services in Springfield will provide assistance in calculating the total fees if necessary.

Illinois Secretary of State   Springfield, IL 62756

Department of Business Services   Telephone (217) 782-9522 or 782-9523

C-162.18

MINUTES OF THE ORGANIZATIONAL MEETING OF THE BOARD OF DIRECTORS
of

_____

Pursuant to Illinois Law, a meeting was held to complete the organization of the corporation. The meeting was held on the _____ day of _____ , at _____ o'clock ___ M. at the principal office of the corporation.

Present at the meeting were the incorporator, and the director(s), officer(s) and shareholder(s) named herein. As evidenced by their attendance and their signatures on the reverse, all directors, officers, and shareholders hereby waive any notice of the meeting that may be required by law. The incorporator duly called the meeting to order and the following items of business were resolved.

DIRECTORS
The incorporator, being all of the incorporators of the corporation, elected the person(s) named below to be director(s) of the corporation until the first annual shareholders meeting at which directors are elected or until new or replace-ment directors are elected. With the duties of the incorporator being completed, the incorporator resigned. A motion was duly made and seconded that the corporation adopt all pre-incorporation transactions entered into by the incorporator. The Chairperson of the Board presided over the remainder of the meeting.

_____   _____
Director   Director

_____   _____
Director   Director

OFFICERS
As their duties are outlined in the corporation bylaws, the Board unanimously elected the following individuals to be officers of the corporation—their respective titles below their name, and their annual salary to the right. These individuals will be officers until which time officers are either reelected or replaced. The president of the corporation was unanimously elected to serve as chairperson of the board of directors. Each person elected to an office accepted their appointment. The president noted that being an officer of the corporation did not preclude officers from holding other salaried positions within the corporation.

_____   _____
President / Chairperson of the Board of Directors   Pres. Salary

_____   _____
Vice-President   V.P. Salary

_____   _____
Secretary   Sec. Salary

_____   _____
Treasurer   Treas. Salary

ARTICLES OF INCORPORATION
A copy of the Articles of Incorporation filed with the State of Illinois on _____ was presented at the meeting. The articles were approved by the directors of the corporation, and it was agreed that the corporate secretary shall place the articles in the corporate records book.

CORPORATE SEAL
The secretary presented at the meeting a proposed corporate seal. After a short discussion, a motion was made and duly seconded that the seal presented at the meeting be adopted as the seal of the corpo-ration. The president noted that the seal shall remain in the custody of the corporate secretary along with the record book of the corporation.

The corporate secretary was directed to place an impression of the seal in the space to the right of this paragraph.

Copyright © 1993 Consumer Publishing, Inc.   CORPORATE SEAL

BYLAWS

A copy of the proposed bylaws for the corporation was presented at the meeting and was considered by the board. Upon motion duly made and seconded it was resolved that the bylaws presented at the meeting shall be the bylaws of the corporation. It was further agreed that the corporate secretary shall include a copy of the bylaws in the corporate records book.

BANK ACCOUNT

The authority by which a bank account may be opened for the corporation is granted by a separate resolution. The corporate secretary was asked to include a copy of that resolution with the corporate records book.

ACCOUNTING PERIOD

Upon motion duly made and seconded it is hereby resolved that the accounting period of the corporation shall end on _____ . It was noted by the president that the corporation must have a December 31 year end to elect IRS Subchapter S status.

ORGANIZATIONAL EXPENSES

After motion duly made and seconded, is was unanimously approved for the corporation to incur, pay, and reimburse any reasonable expenses related to the formation of the corporation. The president noted that organizational expenses of the corporation must be amortized over a period of 60 months.

STOCK

The stock of the corporation was issued under the direction of the Board of Directors. The members of the Board stated that they believe all State and Federal requirements relating to the issuance of the stock of the corporation have been met. Accordingly, a notice that the stock of the corporation is unregistered shall be placed on the certificates. The Board further stated that the stock shall be offered as Section 1244 stock and the issuance shall meet the requirements of IRS Section 1244. The president noted that by meeting the qualifications of IRS Section 1244, shareholders will receive preferential tax treatment in the event of a loss in the value of their stock. Verbal offers to purchase stock in the corporation were made by the individuals listed below and accepted by the Board of Directors. The individuals stated that the shares of stock were purchased for their own account and would not be traded publicly. The corporate secretary presented a stock certificate form at the meeting and it was approved by the board. The secretary will issue certificates to each shareholder and impress the corporate seal on the face of each certificate. Certificates will be signed by the President and Secretary of the Corporation.

Name	No. of Shares	% Ownership	Payment Given *
Name	No. of Shares	% Ownership	Payment Given *
Name	No. of Shares	% Ownership	Payment Given *
Name	No. of Shares	% Ownership	Payment Given *

* If needed, payment may be listed on a separate sheet of paper.

_____
Signature of Corporate Secretary

_____
Date

SIGNATURES OF THOSE IN ATTENDANCE AT THIS MEETING AND NAMED AS A DIRECTOR, OFFICER OR SHAREHOLDER:

_____

_____

_____

_____

Copyright © 1993 Consumer Publishing, Inc.

SHARES

NUMBER

This Certifies that

registered holder of

is the

Shares

transferable only on the books of the Corporation by the holder hereof in person or by Attorney upon surrender of this Certificate properly endorsed.

In Witness Whereof, the said Corporation has caused this Certificate to be signed by its duly authorized officers and its Corporate Seal to be hereunto affixed this _____ day of _____ A.D. 19 _____

© 1994 GOES KG3

For Value Received, _____ hereby sell, assign and transfer

unto _____

_____ Shares

represented by the within Certificate, and do hereby

irrevocably constitute and appoint

_____ Attorney

to transfer the said Shares on the books of the within named

Corporation with full power of substitution in the premises.

Dated _____ 19___

In presence of

_____

_____

NOTICE. THE SIGNATURE OF THIS ASSIGNMENT MUST CORRESPOND WITH THE NAME AS WRITTEN UPON THE FACE OF THE CERTIFICATE, IN EVERY PARTICULAR, WITHOUT ALTERATION OR ENLARGEMENT OR ANY CHANGE WHATEVER.

NUMBER

SHARES

This Certifies that

registered holder of

is the

Shares

transferable only on the books of the Corporation by the holder hereof in person or by Attorney upon surrender of this Certificate properly endorsed.

In Witness Whereof, the said Corporation has caused this Certificate to be signed by its duly authorized officers and its Corporate Seal to be hereunto affixed this _____ day of _____ A.D. 19 _____

© 1994 GOES KG3

For Value Received, _____ *hereby sell, assign and transfer unto* _____

_____ *Shares represented by the within Certificate, and do hereby irrevocably constitute and appoint*

_____ *Attorney to transfer the said Shares on the books of the within named Corporation with full power of substitution in the premises.*

Dated _____ *19* ____

In presence of

_____

_____

NOTICE. THE SIGNATURE OF THIS ASSIGNMENT MUST CORRESPOND WITH THE NAME AS WRITTEN UPON THE FACE OF THE CERTIFICATE, IN EVERY PARTICULAR, WITHOUT ALTERATION OR ENLARGEMENT OR ANY CHANGE WHATEVER.

NOTICE. THE SIGNATURE OF THIS ASSIGNMENT MUST CORRESPOND WITH THE NAME AS WRITTEN UPON THE FACE OF THE CERTIFICATE, IN EVERY PARTICULAR, WITHOUT ALTERATION OR ENLARGEMENT, OR ANY CHANGE WHATEVER.

For Value Received, ——— _hereby sell, assign and transfer_

unto ————————————————————

———————————————————————

Shares represented by the within Certificate, and do hereby

irrevocably constitute and appoint ——————————

Attorney

to transfer the said Shares on the books of the within named

Corporation with full power of substitution in the premises.

Dated ——————— _19___

———————————

In presence of

NUMBER

SHARES

This Certifies that

registered holder of

is the Shares

transferable only on the books of the Corporation by the holder hereof in person or by Attorney upon surrender of this Certificate properly endorsed.

In Witness Whereof, the said Corporation has caused this Certificate to be signed by its duly authorized officers and its Corporate Seal to be hereunto affixed this _____ day of _____ A.D. 19 _____.

© 1994 GOES KG3

For Value Received, _____ hereby sell, assign and transfer unto _____

_____ Shares represented by the within Certificate, and do hereby irrevocably constitute and appoint

_____ Attorney to transfer the said Shares on the books of the within named Corporation with full power of substitution in the premises.

Dated _____ 19____

In presence of

_____

_____

NOTICE. THE SIGNATURE OF THIS ASSIGNMENT MUST CORRESPOND WITH THE NAME AS WRITTEN UPON THE FACE OF THE CERTIFICATE, IN EVERY PARTICULAR, WITHOUT ALTERATION OR ENLARGEMENT OR ANY CHANGE WHATEVER.

...*Our Business Library*

The Incorporating Without A Lawyer Series

Incorporating is a routine procedure that basically consists of putting your name and address on a standard form, holding a meeting, and issuing stock. Our books will show you the quickest and easiest way to incorporate your business in any of 33 states—including the popular state of Nevada. They'll lead you step-by-step through the incorporating process of either a C or an S corporation, and come complete with ready-to-use forms and genuine GOES® stock certificates.

Available States:

AL	AR	AZ	CA	CO	CT
DC	FL	GA	IL	IN	KS
KY	MA	MD	MI	MN	MO
MS	NC	NJ	NY	NV	OH
OK	OR	PA	TN	TX	UT
VA	WA	WI			

A Delaware book is also available. Please see *How to Form Your Own Corporation Without a Lawyer for Less Than $75* on page two.

—*incorporating made easy* $24.⁹⁵

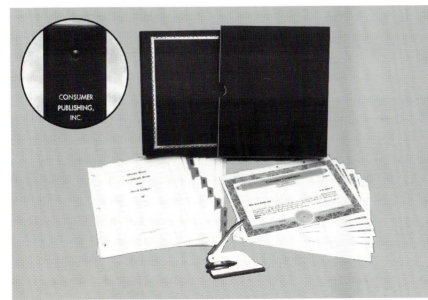

Standard Corporate Outfit

Well kept records are the sign of a properly organized corporation and can protect its legal status. To store your corporate records, we offer the finest corporate record books available. Personalized especially for you, this outfit features a sturdy, handsomely designed 3-ring binder with your corporate name embossed in gold on the spine. It is made from a rich, leather grained vinyl and comes with a matching slipcase.

Also included:

- A heavy duty, chrome–plated seal engraved with your corporate name, state and year of incorporation.

- 20 numbered stock certificates custom printed with the corporate name and a stock transfer ledger.

- Preprinted minutes, medical & dental reimbursement plan, Subchapter S forms, Section 1244 forms, and annual meeting forms.

—*O ring binder in black, green, or tan* $63.⁰⁰
—*D ring binder, black with burgundy trim* $68.⁰⁰

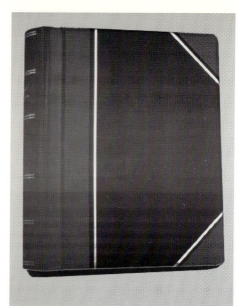

Deluxe Corporate Outfit

This beautiful outfit includes everything that our standard kit does with a deluxe black & burgundy binder that looks and feels like real leather. It features a rounded library spine–gold embossed with your corporate name, triple post binding and a matching slip case. It is also available in green or black–with a gold border on the front.

—all seals and outfits ship within 24 hours .... $89.^{00}

Leather Corporate Outfit

This beautiful outfit includes everything that our Deluxe kit does with a genuine leather binder.

—Available in black or burgundy. .... $199.^{00}

Seal Only

The same high quality chrome–plated corporate seal available with our kits is available alone. The seal is engraved with the name of your corporation, the state and date of incorporation.

—next day service is available .... $30.^{00}

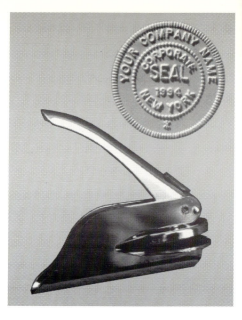

Taking Care of Your Corporation
shows you how to take care of day-to-day corporate business and comply with state law requirements for keeping corporate records. It explains how to hold corporate meetings, keep and prepare corporate minutes, pass board and shareholder resolutions, legally document corporate transactions, amend articles and bylaws, prepare buy/sell provisions to control the sale of corporate stock and more.

—for corporate secretaries. .... $26.^{95}

How to Form your Own Corporation w/o a Lawyer for Less Than $75
In its 20th edition, this book has incorporated more businesses than any other. If you want to incorporate in Delaware, this is the book for you. It has everything you need including the certificate of incorporation, minutes, bylaws and step-by-step instructions.

—the Delaware book .... $19.^{95}

The Essential Corporation Handbook
An "owner's manual" for your corporation, this book explains all the hows and whys of corporations. It covers everything from incorporating to dissolution. Subjects include—piercing of the corporate veil, shareholder buy/sell agreements, securities law, the roles of officers and directors, mergers, bylaws, proxies and more. It also includes checklists to properly form and maintain your corp.

—an owners manual for your corp. .... $19.^{95}

Stand Up To The IRS
is a hands on guide to battling the IRS and coaxing favorable decisions from agency personnel. It shows you how to defend yourself in an audit, challenge an incorrect tax bill, negotiate an installment plan, appeal an audit decision, file delinquent tax returns, support your deductions, and represent yourself in tax court. "Best personal finance book", says *Money Magazine*.

—a necessity for CPA's. .... $21.^{95}

A Guide to Limited Liability Companies
provides a short but thorough discussion on this popular new form of business entity. It includes a historical overview, explores the formation and accounting, transferring interest, Federal and state tax treatment of LLC's and much more. It also compares LLC's with partnerships and Subchapter S corporations.

176 pages .... $29.^{95}

How to Form a Nonprofit Corporation
explains everything you need to know to start and operate a nonprofit corporation. A special appendix includes the specific requirements for incorporating your organization in your state. It also includes complete instructions for obtaining tax–exempt and public charity status with the IRS.

—instructions for all 50 states .... $39.^{95}

Plan Your Estate With a Living Trust
is simply the most comprehensive guide to estate planning available. It covers topics from basic planning to sophisticated tax saving strategies. It's the only book that shows you how to create an estate plan tailored to your needs. Good in all states except Louisiana. Includes durable powers of attorney, and living wills too!

—a complete handbook .... $24.^{95}

Business Owners Guide to Accounting & Bookkeeping
is a nontechnical, easy to understand book that will teach you the basics of accounting and how to keep your own books. Not only will it teach you how to prepare your own financial statements, but it'll also show you how to make them look their best for creditors.

—accounting made easy .... $19.^{95}

There's one for your state too!

The Legal Guide for Starting & Running a Small Business
This book is a must-have comprehensive legal handbook for entrepreneurs. It covers all areas of operating a business including corporations, partnerships, business purchases, contracts, licenses, permits, leases, contractors, hiring & firing, customers, ind. contractors, insurance, taxes and more.

—your own desktop lawyer $24.⁹⁵

The Home Based Entrepreneur
This all new and fully updated edition covers everything you'll need to know to legally operate your business from home. This book will show you how to deal with zoning, labor laws, licenses & how to make the most of tax deductions for your home office.

—for home offices $19.⁹⁵

Keeping What's Yours
Today's lawsuit explosion makes every business person vulnerable to costly legal claims. This book is the insider's guide to asset protection and will show you how to legally and ethically protect yourself and your property from lawsuits. Among other strategies, it shows how to use your corporation and trusts to protect what's yours. The title says it all…

—protect your assets $19.⁹⁵

Starting & Operating a Business Series
is the best one-stop resource to *current* state and Federal regulations that affect your business. It'll help you cut through the red tape in your state and get you started off on the right foot. It includes extensive checklists and information on permits, licenses, business taxes, insurance, employees, payroll & unemployment taxes, workers comp., and more.

—please specify state $24.⁹⁵

Trademark—How to Name Your Business & Product
is by far the best comprehensive do-it-yourself trademark book available—a user friendly guide to the laws that govern commercial names. This book will show you how to choose a name competitors can't copy, conduct a trademark search, register your trademark with the U.S. Patent and Trademark office, protect your trademark from infringement and more.

—protect your name $29.⁹⁵

Patent it Yourself
contains all the forms and specific step-by-step instructions that you'll need to patent your invention in the United States. It explains the entire process from the patent search to the actual application. It also covers use and licensing, marketing of your invention and how to deal with infringement.

—save a small fortune $39.⁹⁵

The Employer's Legal Handbook
This is the most comprehensive resource available that covers your questions about hiring, firing, and everything in between. Its 350 pages include topics like—discrimination, privacy rights, employee rights, workplace health and safety, employee benefits, wages, hours, tips and commissions, sexual harassment, termination, taxes, liability insurance, and safe hiring practices.

—stay out of court $29.⁹⁵

How to Write a Business Plan
Your banker, investors, and the Small Business Administration need your business plan, but where do you start? Used by SBA offices around the country, this 272 page best-seller comes complete with examples, forms, and work sheets that show you how to write a winning business plan in only *one* day. It will help you present your business opportunity to bankers and investors in a format they'll understand.

—finish your business plan in a day $19.⁹⁵

How to Form Your Own New York Corporation
This 272 page book will lead you step-by-step through the incorporating process in New York. Not only does it have everything you'll need, but the forms are also included on a DOS 3 1/2" disk.

Book, and disk $39.⁹⁵

How to Form Your Own Texas Corporation
This 240 page book will lead you step-by-step through the incorporating process in Texas. It not only has all the forms that you'll need but also includes the forms on a DOS 3 1/2" disk.

Book, and disk $39.⁹⁵

How to Form Your Own Florida Corporation
This 225 page book will lead you step-by-step through the incorporating process in Florida. Not only does it have everything you'll need, but the forms are also included on a 3 1/2" DOS disk.

Book, and disk $39.⁹⁵

How to Form Your Own California Corporation
includes a 288 page step-by-step incorporating guide and a 3.5" IBM disk with all the forms you'll need. Included to keep your corporate papers organized is a corporate records binder that includes 10 stock certificates, and indexed dividers.

Binder, book & disk $39.⁹⁵

Order Form

ORDERING OPTIONS

1. *Call* us at 1-800-677-2462 and place your order using a Visa or MasterCard.

2. *Fax* your order, credit card number and expiration date to 1-423-539-6600

3. *Mail* your order with a personal check, business check, money order or credit card information to:

Consumer Publishing, Inc.
P.O. Box 23830
Concord, TN 37933-1830

RETURNS

Your satisfaction is guaranteed. We only ask that books be returned in saleable condition within 30 days. Software must be unopened.

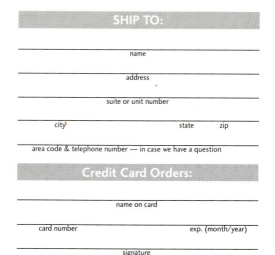

SHIP TO:

_____
name

_____
address

_____
suite or unit number

_____
city   state   zip

_____
area code & telephone number — in case we have a question

Credit Card Orders:

_____
name on card

_____
card number   exp. (month/year)

_____
signature

SHIPPING OPTIONS

Books—We ship books via U.S. Priority Mail unless you need overnight delivery.

Priority Mail arrives in 2-3 days and costs $3 for the first book and $1 for each additional book.

Federal Express arrives the next day and charges depend on the weight of the book(s). Please call for Fed Ex rates.

Corporate outfits and seals are shipped within 24 hours by UPS unless you request overnight delivery. Overnight orders must be placed before 2 pm Eastern time.

The UPS charge is $4 per item. Overnight delivery via Airborne Express is $9 per item. *A street address is required for delivery of corporate outfits and seals.*

Books & Software

Quant.	Description		Price Ea.	Total
	A Guide to Limited Liability Companies		29.95	
	Business Owners Guide to Accounting and Bookkeeping		19.95	
	How to Form a Nonprofit Corporation		39.95	
	How to Form Your Own Corporation w/o a Lawyer for Less than $75—Delaware		19.95	
	How to Form Your Own CALIFORNIA Corporation—book, binder and DOS 3.5 inch disk.		39.95	
	How to Form Your Own NEW YORK Corporation—book, and DOS 3.5 inch disk.		39.95	
	How to Form Your Own TEXAS Corporation—book, and DOS 3.5 inch disk.		39.95	
	How to Form Your Own FLORIDA Corporation—book, and DOS 3.5 inch disk.		39.95	
	How to Write a Business Plan		19.95	
	Keeping What's Yours		19.95	
	Patent it Yourself		39.95	
	Plan Your Estate With a Living Trust		24.95	
	Stand Up to the IRS		21.95	
	Starting & Operating a Business Series	— *specify state(s)*:	24.95	
	Taking Care of Your Corporation		26.95	
	The Employer's Legal Handbook		29.95	
	The Essential Corporation Handbook		19.95	
	The Home Based Entrepreneur		19.95	
	The Incorporating Without a Lawyer series	— *specify state(s)*:	24.95	
	The Legal Guide for Starting and Running a Small Business		24.95	
	Trademark, How to Name Your Business & Product		29.95	
	Blank Stock Certificates—specify gold, green, or blue	package of 10 certificates	5.00	

Corporate Supplies

Quant.	Description					Price Ea.	Total
	Standard Corporate Outfit	—*circle color*	black	tan (camel)	green	63.00	
	Standard Corporate Outfit—D ring binder in black/burgundy					68.00	
	Deluxe Corporate Outfit	—*circle color*	black/burg.	black	green	89.00	
	Leather Corporate outfit					199.00	
	Seal Only					30.00	

Prices are current as of 11/1/95, and may be subject to change.

Corporate Information

_____
corporate name as it will appear on the outfit — either ALL CAPS - Initial Caps - or any combination of caps and lower case letters.

_____
date of inc.   state of inc.   number of AUTHORIZED shares   par value   is it common stock ?

Subtotal _____

(*TN residents only*) Sales tax _____

Shipping _____

Total _____